PHOTO GUIDE

COLOGNE

The Rhine is Cologne's main artery, and the cathedral is its heart. The cityscape is particularly beautiful at night when you gaze from the Deutz Bridge to Gross St Martin and the cathedral.

Pope Leo IX called the town "Holy Cologne" in 1052. The fantastic architecture reminds servers at Mass in the cathedral of the traditions of their faith.

ABOUT THIS BOOK

"We spent an hour in the cathedral, which I will not attempt to describe further than by saying it was the most beautiful of all the churches I have ever seen, or can imagine. If one could imagine the spirit of devotion embodied in any material form, it would be in such a building."

Lewis Carroll's diary, July 1867

Cologne's philosophy of life can be summed up in two sentences: "Et kütt, wie et kütt" (in the words of the popular song, "Que sera, sera" or "Whatever will be, will be") and "Et hätt noch immer jot jejange" ("It'll be fine"). This cathedral town takes things as they come, convinced that everything will turn out for the best. Such civic nonchalance comes after two thousand years of history: the locals saw off the Romans, just as they survived occupation by the French in the 19th century.

Cologne is rightly proud of its cultural variety. It encompasses both the ancient treasures of the Roman-Germanic Museum and the no-less fascinating modernity of the Museum Ludwig, while the range of music on offer starts with the lowly busking violinist and continues beyond the climax of a concert by the Philharmonic. The exceptional significance of the cathedral and the Romanesque churches has led UNESCO to declare the city a World Heritage Site. Traditional culture is also valued highly by the people of Cologne: they hold Kölsch in as high esteem as Kölsch the dialect, and the Carnival is a cultural phenomenon apart, celebrated as enthusiastically on the banks of the Rhine as it is beside the Sugar Loaf Mountain.

Cologne is one of a new and unique series. *Photo Guides* combine the lavishness of a coffee-table book with the practicality of a travel guide to create the perfect companion for your city visit. There are over 400 high-quality photographs and maps, together with comprehensive information about the essential highlights of the city and its festivals and lifestyle, district by district. Features about the city's history and local culture are accompanied by a detailed timeline, guided walks with tips from the experts on shopping and eating, information about the major museums and, of course, all the essential addresses. Each *Photo Guide* also includes a detailed city atlas to help you find your way about.

Note: In the German language "ss" can also be written as "ß" – you will find examples of both in this book.

What Cologne girl doesn't dream of being "Funkenmariechen" (Carnival Queen) for the procession on Rose Monday, the day before Lent? For the people of Cologne, Carnival is an important part of local culture and collective identity.

TIMELINE

THE HIGHLIGHTS

CONTENTS

This book consists of four parts. The Timeline gives a comprehensive account of the city's past. The Highlights section reveals the city's treasures with stunning photographs, local maps, ideas for places to eat, and special features. The City Explorer gives the insider's knowledge, district by district, of culture, shopping, eating and drinking, accommodation, and seasonal events; it also presents the best museums and fantastic city walks. And, finally, the City Atlas will ensure you find your way around with ease.

CITY EXPLORER

CITY ATLAS

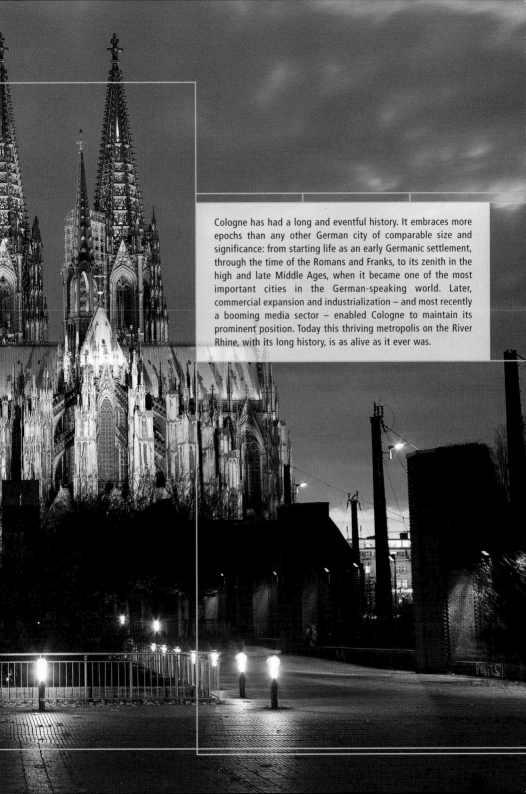

Cologne has had a long and eventful history. It embraces more epochs than any other German city of comparable size and significance: from starting life as an early Germanic settlement, through the time of the Romans and Franks, to its zenith in the high and late Middle Ages, when it became one of the most important cities in the German-speaking world. Later, commercial expansion and industrialization – and most recently a booming media sector – enabled Cologne to maintain its prominent position. Today this thriving metropolis on the River Rhine, with its long history, is as alive as it ever was.

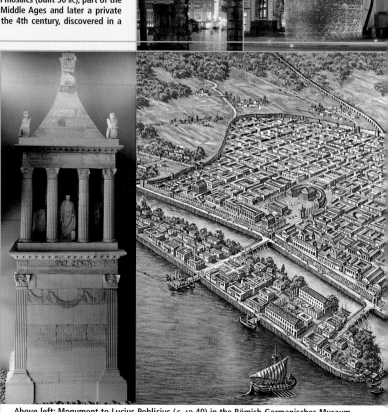

From left: The remains of the Roman north gate (2nd century BC), originally part of the city wall, on Cathedral Square with a view of the Hohe Strasse; the so-called Roman Tower, which is a watchtower decorated with mosaics (built 50 BC), part of the Poor Clares' convent in the Middle Ages and later a private dwelling; sarcophagus from the 4th century, discovered in a grave chamber in Weiden.

39–38 BC
The Roman General Marcus Vipsanius Agrippa establishes a camp for two legions on the left bank of the Rhine and resettles members of the Germanic Ubii tribe here.

circa **AD 90**
Colonia Claudia Ara Agrippinensium (CCAA) becomes capital of the province of Germania Inferior.

3rd century
First Christian groups in Cologne; docks area filled in (now Old Town).

circa **310**
First permanent bridge to right bank of Rhine constructed; construction of fort at Divitia (Deutz).

313
Documentary evidence of earliest known Bishop, Maternus, called to a synod in Rome by Emperor Constantine.

355
Franks and Alemanni loot Cologne; 366 reconquest by Rome.

401/405
The West Roman military commander Flavius Stilicho evacuates his last troops from the Rheinland; the Romans leave Cologne.

460
Cologne becomes a Frankish power base; the kings of the Ripuarian Franks now sit in state in the residence of the former Roman governor.

Above left: Monument to Lucius Poblicius (*c.* AD 40) in the Römisch-Germanisches Museum.
Above right: Reconstruction of the city by E. Saalfeld: Roman Cologne could well have looked like this around AD 200.

The Romans in Cologne

Cologne is among the nobility of Germany's cities, even if it was founded by the Romans. Around 50 BC, as part of the conquest of Gaul, Caesar's legions depopulated the left bank of the Rhine so comprehensively that the way was made clear for the settlement of the more Roman-friendly Ubii people from the right bank. At the behest of his wife, Agrippina, Emperor Claudius secured the town's future in 50 BC by declaring it a retirement colony for veterans. He called it Colonia Claudia Ara Agrippinensium, or CCAA for short. It was an image of the "eternal city" in the provinces, complete with an imperial altar, a Capitol building, a city wall and a grid street network. Forty years later, Cologne became the capital of Germania Inferior. The governor resided in the Praetorium and indulgently watched his "Colonia" develop into a commercial hub of glass-making north of the Alps. The Franks began harassing the legions in the middle of the 3rd century, and one general even declared a short-lived independent empire, ruled from Cologne. In 310 the Romans bridged the Rhine and erected a fort at Divitia (now Deutz). Even this did not prevent the Franks and Alemanni from sacking Cologne in 355, and 50 years later the Romans abandoned the Rhineland to its fate; Frankish kings moved into the Praetorium.

Agrippina the Younger

Julia Agrippina was strong, proud, and avaricious, and had her husband, Emperor Claudius, under her thumb. She had no qualms about using poison to remove him in AD 54, to make way for Domitius, her 17-year-old son from her first marriage, and thus also to install herself as his chief adviser. This is what the Roman historian Tacitus tells us (elsewhere he heartily recommends the robust nature of the Germans as an example to his etiolated, decadent compatriots). From the very beginning, Agrippina had the closest connections to the imperial household. Her parents were the Roman general Germanicus, a great-nephew of Augustus, the first Caesar, and Agrippina the Elder, who herself was the daughter of the great general Agrippa. He had cleared Augustus' route to power, married his daughter Julia, and settled the people of Ubii where Cologne stands today.

Agrippina was born in AD 15 in the Oppidum Ubiorum, when her parents were visiting the Rhine. Among her eight siblings was the future emperor (AD 37–41) Caligula, who has gone down in history as an insane despot. During her rise to power, Agrippina encountered a setback when her own brother banished her from Rome, just as Emperor Tiberius had banished her mother ten years previously. However, she was recalled by her uncle, Claudius, who had been elevated to the throne when Caligula was murdered by the Praetorian Guard.

After a short marriage to one Passenius Crispius, she became Claudius' fourth wife at the age of 49. Such a union between uncle and niece was a scandal, but Agrippina overcame all resistance to the idea. Nevertheless, becoming the wife of the emperor was not enough: the Senate bestowed the honorary title "Augusta" upon her, emphasizing her equality with Claudius, the emperor, who was putty in her hands in any case. He adopted her son – Domitius Ahenobarbus, who became Nero Claudius – and turned the town of her birth into a model colony. Uniquely, the inhabitants took to calling themselves after a woman, when they described themselves as "Agrippinense". Thus Agrippina's own name was immortalized, but she herself was not to live much longer. Nero had barely been emperor for five years when he sought to escape his mother's suffocating care, and he knew of no better method than to have her murdered. Although he was responsible for the deed, it happened (once again) at the behest of a woman: Octavia, Nero's wife and Claudius' daughter from his first marriage to Messalina. What a drama!

Contemporary marble statue of Agrippina the Younger, who gave her name to Cologne.

From left: Interior of the Romanesque church Gross St Martin, the construction of which was begun in the 12th century on Roman foundations; a view of the interior of the basilica of the modern-day parish church of St Gereon; the crypt of St Maria im Kapitol; St Maria's apse.

794/795
Charlemagne elevates Cologne to an archdiocese, appointing his adviser Hildebold (a bishop since 787) the first incumbent.

870
Consecration of the Carolingian cathedral.

953
Expansion of the city and construction of Gross St Martin by Archbishop Bruno, brother of Otto the Great.

1028
The Archbishop of Cologne receives the right to crown the Roman-German king (at Aachen).

1074
Suppression of revolt by Cologne citizens against Archbishop Anno II.

1164
Removal of the remains of the Three Kings to Cologne by Archbishop Rainald von Dassel.

1176
Formation of a trade partnership (Hanse) by Cologne merchants; the city acquires the "staple right" from 1150.

1248
Foundation stone of the new High Gothic cathedral laid in emulation of the Carolingian cathedral.

1288
Defeat of Archbishop Siegfried von Westerburg by the citizens of Cologne in the Battle of Worringen.

Sancta Colonia

When Cologne appointed itself the "true daughter of the Roman Church by God's grace" (*Sancta colonia dei gracia romane ecclesie fidelis filia*), as Germany's largest medieval town with 4,000 inhabitants it was seeking to compete with the greatest cities in Christendom: Rome and Constantinople. The people of Cologne had every reason for self-confidence. Their Christian community had a long tradition, having been founded in the 3rd century; their archbishops had crowned and advised every German king since 1028; their merchants were rich, trade was flourishing, and Cologne artisans were producing work of the highest quality.

Yet, above all this, it was Cologne's churches, with their countless relics of saints, and martyrs, as well as other witnesses of faith, that attracted visitors in their tens of thousands. The most famous relics, both then and now, are St Peter's chains and pastoral staff and the remains of the Three Kings, which were looted from Milan as war booty by Archbishop Rainald von Dassel, chancellor to Emperor Frederick Barbarossa.

Anyone undertaking a pilgrimage to Cologne for the good of their soul would have been rewarded with entering a city in the image of the heavenly New Jerusalem that awaits the faithful after the Last Judgement. Even from a distance, the imposing sight of St Gereon, a basilica with the third-largest cupola in Western Christendom (after the Duomo in Florence and the Hagia Sophia in Constantinople), would have reinforced the pilgrim's faith. The frescoes and mosaics, the imposing shrines, and the graceful statuary in the twelve large Romanesque churches and an even greater number of parish churches, seminaries, and monasteries would have transported the pilgrim into a world of Bible stories and holy legend. Who could doubt that bones harvested from ancient cemeteries were those of St Ursula's 11,000-strong female retinue or of Theban legionaries, executed for their beliefs?

The pilgrims and general population of Cologne were not alone in their desire for prayer and redemption; the words of Cologne scholars carried great weight, especially those of Albertus Magnus (c. 1200–1280), and the mendicant Dominican and Franciscan orders, who maintained important theological seminaries that were the forerunners of the university to be founded later, in 1388.

The reverse of the Three Kings' Shrine in Cologne Cathedral: Archbishop Rainald von Dassel was chancellor to Emperor Barbarossa and a powerful man in the 12th century.

The Gothic cathedral

The High Gothic cathedral, St Peter und St Marien (St Peter and St Mary) was built to house the bones of the Three Kings. The architecture of this archdiocesan church was intended to abandon the earthbound heaviness of the Romanesque style; the Gothic design of the building, its proportions and columns dissolving into the heavens from spaces flooded with light, was to give believers a foretaste of redemption. Pilgrims were also to be inspired by the story of the Adoration of Christ by the Magi, one of the cathedral's principal motifs. By the time building work started on the church, France had already introduced the Gothic style, and its cathedrals were to serve as inspirational models. The French king's royal chapel in Paris, the Sainte-Chapelle, was completed in 1248, the year Archbishop Konrad von Hochstaden laid the foundation stone for Cologne's cathedral. St Peter und St Marien was constructed with five naves and the choir chevet was completed by 1265, incorporating seven apsidal chapels. The roof arches over the choir were completed in 1300 and the apse was consecrated on 27 September 1322, allowing Holy Mass to be celebrated and the cathedral authorities to return their attention to worldly things. The belfry of the south tower received its first bells in the 15th century, but building work stopped soon after, through lack of funds, and the edifice was completed only in 1880.

The cathedral's central nave is 43.25 m (143 feet) high.

From left: The late Romanesque Overstolzenhaus is now the home of the Media College; the old Town Hall (1330, tower 1407–1414) has taken on the appearance of a Renaissance building since the addition of the so-called Town Hall loggia in 1569; imposing statues of apostles (cathedral detail); the Gürzenich was built between 1441 and 1447, and is used as a function hall (steel engraving by Gürzenich, *c.* 1850).

1288–1396
Dynastic rule (by a corporation of patricians): the "narrow council" (15 members); 1318 formation of the "great council" (82 members).

1317
King Edward II of England confirms the trading rights and privileges of Cologne merchants.

1330
Reconstruction of the Town Hall, a symbol of the patricians' independence from the archbishop.

24. August 1349
St Bartholomew's Day: pogroms of Jews, blamed for the Black Death.

1369–1371
The insurrection of weavers against patrician rule.

1396–1794
Patrician dynastic rule toppled: guilds take control.

1404
Jews prohibited from wearing jewellery and "conspicuous" clothing.

1407–1414
Erection of Town Hall tower by guilds, a symbol of victory over the patricians.

1441–1447
Construction of Gürzenich: coronation ceremonies and a Diet (the legislature of the empire) take place in the hall.

1471–1476
Cologne excluded from the Hanse.

The Old Market in Cologne is one of the city's hubs. The buildings in this historic view clearly betray the influence of Renaissance sensibilities.

Cologne, city of commerce

The citizens of Cologne took municipal control of their city after the Battle of Worringen in 1288, although Cologne's highest

The Battle of Worringen (manuscript illustration).

court of appeal remained the consistory court led by the archbishop until the

French occupation of 1794. Initially, rich patrician families ensured power for themselves alone, but when the "Verbundbrief", a sort of democratic constitution, passed into law in 1396 power was transferred to the guilds, the associations of tradesmen and merchants in the city. From then on the town council was composed of 36 guild representatives, elected for a year by the enfranchised male citizens who made up about a third of the city's population. The inhabitants of Cologne owed their self-assurance and influence to the growing international and commercial importance of their town. Cologne had been a member of the Hanse since the 12th century and specialist production techniques and increasing trade meant that the city could boast a range of wares that was being

sold right across Europe. Its trade links stretched north to Tallinn on the Baltic and Bergen in Norway, and south to Lisbon and Sicily. Precious silks, spices, and incense of oriental origin reached the Rhine via Milan and Venice; iron, vellum, furs, and skins came via Danzig (now Gdansk) and Lübeck. The city specialized in exporting rare cloths, fur, and leather. The turnover within Cologne was also considerable and there was no lack of clients with buying power; the high-ranking clerics joined their wealthy patrician counterparts in ensuring a healthy demand for luxury goods of all kinds. Churches and monasteries were fitted out with extravagant interiors and reliquaries were fashioned for the relics, much to the benefit of local gold- and silversmiths. The textile industry experienced

The Rhine quays and staple yard with the church of Gross St Martin (steel engraving by Joseph Maximilian Kolb, c. 1850).

The seal of the University, founded in 1388, one of the first municipal places of learning on German soil.

a similar boom: senior clergy had always preferred only the finest materials for clerical garb, and elaborately woven silk garments, filigreed with gold and silver thread, soon began to suit the taste of the rich citizenry.

The banishment of the Jews in the High Middle Ages represents a dark chapter in the city's history. Separated from the rest of the town, the oldest Jewish community in Germany had lived in a ghetto on the Brüdergasse, the Kleine Budengasse, the Portalsgasse, and the Jerusalemgässchen. Its central buildings were the synagogue and the mikvah, the ritual bathhouse, which were as tall as the modern Town Hall. Many Jews had risen to positions of wealth as pawnbrokers and gold merchants, both professions proscribed for Christians. This was a situation of great

irritation to some sections of the populace, and the pogroms that had been carried out against this religious minority in the wake of the First Crusade in the 11th century were to be repeated 300 years later, principally as a response to the arrival of the Black Death in Cologne. Although the archbishops repeatedly placed the Jewish community under their especial protection, they were unable to resolve the prejudice and envy, and the antipathy of some inhabitants reached a further crescendo in the 14th and 15th centuries. Initially, they found an outlet for their hatred in renewed pogroms, but in 1424 Jews were banished from the city altogether. Many families subsequently settled in Deutz, on the other side of the Rhine, in order to continue trading with Cologne merchants.

Staple right

Cologne had its own wealth and economic growth in the High Middle Ages to thank for its acquisition of the so-called "staple right" in 1259. Early in its history, the city had developed into a staging post for goods of all kinds, and the staple right obliged all merchants passing through to store their wares there, offering them for sale to Cologne merchants for a period of three days. During this time, trade with merchants from out of town was strictly prohibited. This especially affected trade on the Rhine – goods bound by staple right included salt, wine, cattle, skins, and leather, as well as timber, stone, and coal. The point of the undertaking was to assure supplies for the city, but it also constituted a sort of quality control; only goods

that were of a certain standard were given a hallmark and then given permission to be transported further and sold.

The necessary delays to business caused by this storage were disadvantageous, however, and many merchants attempted to evade the staple right by smuggling their goods past Cologne; the so-called "Mauspfad" (mouse path) skirting the Bergisches Land gained some notoriety for this practice.

Over the course of the centuries, ever-greater numbers of traders took to avoiding Cologne and the city's turnover of goods dropped continuously as a result. Nonetheless, Cologne continued to cling to the staple right and it was only after the Rhine Shipping Acts of 1831 that it was finally abolished and goods could pass freely.

From left: "Witches cooking up wind and rain", a woodcut produced in Cologne in 1489; Friedrich Spee von Langenfeld (1591–1635), a Jesuit who took part in the witch trials; "The Triumph of Doctor Reuchlin", a woodcut from 1518 depicting the philosopher and humanist Johannes Reuchlin (1455–1522) in his struggle against anti-Jewish activity by the citizens of Cologne.

1475
Emperor Frederick III confers the status of Free Imperial City after the War of Neuss.

1482
First of a series of revolts against the authorities; attempts by citizens and guilds to recover their chartered rights succeed only in 1512.

1505/1512
The Diet convened in Cologne on these two occasions only.

1542–1547
Archbishop Hermann V von Wied fails to introduce the Reformation.

1544
The Council allows the Jesuits to settle in Cologne (1582 construction of the Jesuit monastery).

1560
Interruption of building work on the cathedral.

1582–1585
Conversion of Archbishop Gebhard II, Steward of Waldburg, to Protestantism; War of Cologne (1583–1588). Subsequent Wittelsbach rule.

1632
Occupation of Deutz by Swedish troops. Cologne escapes the Thirty Years War unscathed.

***circa* 1700**
Invention of Kölnisch Wasser – Eau de Cologne.

Cologne around 1531; right, the eternal building site of the cathedral (woodcut).

Beholden only to God and the Emperor

By the end of the 15th century the council of Cologne was in imperial favor. In thanks for Cologne's support in the War of Neuss (1474–1475) against the Duke of Burgundy, the Habsburg ruler Frederick III had solemnly conferred upon it the status of Free Imperial City. This meant that Cologne was not part of any other territory, and was beholden to no other ruler than the Emperor of the Holy Roman Empire of the German Nation, who had also seen fit to relieve the city of any burden of taxation. As a result the City Council, in whom all local power resided, was answerable to none.

The council members' awareness of Cologne's essential importance, which was confirmed through the honor of a series of imperial visits (in 1486, 1488, and 1494) and the convocation of two Diets in 1505 and 1512, seems to have made them increasingly arrogant and deaf to the cares and concerns of the city's inhabitants. The Council sought to make good its expenses after the War of Neuss through increased taxation and excise duty. The guilds and citizens were angered by this and resisted the charges – initially in vain, but eventually they were successful: in 1512 both mayors and a number of burgesses met their end under the executioner's axe. Nonetheless, even after 1512, the money and connections of the burgesses and enfranchised families ensured

that they still retained greater political leverage throughout the 16th and early 17th centuries. Any struggle against them meant questioning the very nature of municipal authority, as Nikolaus Gülich discovered in his doomed attempt to fight corruption in the City Hall and establish a just administration. The city leader fought back and the crowds could only watch as the fighter for justice was deprived of both his honor and his head on the scaffold in 1686.

However, during this period, the question of authority was also being raised in a very different context: that of the spiritual world. The City Council was vehemently opposed to the introduction of Luther's Reformation – and the cathedral officials, fearful

Nikolaus Gülich

Nikolaus Gülich was executed on Mülheim heath on 23 November 1686. No one can now say for sure whether the last thing he saw was the left bank of the Rhine, where he had sought justice for himself and for so many of his fellow-citizens, but, in the eyes of later supporters of the French Revolution, a true revolutionary died that day. Gülich had had a manufacturing business, and he blamed its failure on the abuses of justice and the law at the hands of the ruling Cologne clique. With the zeal of a lawyer, and at the head of a Protestant popular movement, he had attempted to expose mismanagement and nepotism, and put an end to "perjury, theft, and fraud". The City Hall was stormed and in 1683 a "clean" Council was elected, but Gülich went too far, trying to extend his reforms further, and eventually he alienated his supporters. After his execution, the Council attempted to steer public memory back in the "right" direction; his house was torn down, an edict was decreed forbidding construction on the site in perpetuity, and a pillar of shame was erected with a bronze of Gülich's head on the top.

Today, this man who was vilified by the City Council is remembered with respect: Cologne's Green Party has even set up the Nikolaus Gülich Fund, intended to promote political initiatives supporting "the dissemination of justice, democracy in action, freedom from violence and human rights".

for their stipends, as well as theologians, fearful for their authority, leapt to their aid. The Dominicans opened hostilities with the humanists by coming down on the side of a Jewish convert to Catholicism, Johannes Pfefferkorn, who had issued a tract in 1510 demanding the burning of all Jewish scripture that did not feature in the Bible. This rather public affair was enough to bring Cologne the reputation of being less than progressive, yet the issue really began to heat up when Gebhard II, Steward of Waldburg and Archbishop of Cologne, not only recanted and joined the Protestants but also attempted to dissolve his archbishopric. Up until this time the city of Cologne had had no real problem with Gebhard II as the temporal lord of the archdiocese and

its properties, but now, supported by Catholic Bavaria, among others, it declared on him what was to become known as the War of Cologne (1583–1588) – and won. The city had already sided with the Catholics in allowing the Jesuits to settle in Cologne in 1544, although, mindful of the sympathy that many citizens had for the Reformation, it was obliged to tread carefully and only recognized the Jesuits as an official order at the end of the 16th century. These "Soldiers of Christ", loyal only to the Pope, settled the city in the Catholic faith, despite its good connections to the Establishment: the process was brought about not through blind dogmatism, but with the application of demanding theology and the establishment of excellent

places of learning. Cologne survived both Reformation and Counter-Reformation largely unscathed, but its boom time as a metropolis of trade and industry was over. Progress lay beyond the medieval city wall.

Clemens August, a Wittelsbach Elector (1723).

From left: View of Cologne around 1855, with the port and storehouses in the foreground. The Town Hall tower can be seen in the far left, next to Gross St Martin, another striking symbol of Cologne, along with the cathedral (seen here without spires). To the right of the cathedral lies St Mariä Himmelfahrt, the former Jesuit church. In the picture on the right, taken 45 years later: the finished cathedral.

6 April 1794
The French occupy Cologne. Its 12,000 inhabitants offer no resistance.

8 April 1796
Introduction of house numbers. The cathedral receives the number 1.

17 November 1797
"Equality of all citizens." Jews and Protestants receive the same rights as Catholics.

28 April 1798
The French issue an edict closing the university.

9 June 1802
As part of the process of secularization, all church property is handed over to the state.

31 March 1831
The Rhine Acts are signed into law, abolishing taxation of river traffic.

10 February 1823
First Rose Monday procession organized by an official committee.

2 August 1839
Opening of the first section of the Cologne-Aachen railway.

4 September 1842
Frederick William IV, King of Prussia, lays the foundation stone for renewed building work on the cathedral.

28 April 1877
Opening of the first horse-drawn tram between Deutz and Kalk.

Breakthrough into modernity

After centuries of decline, the city of Cologne at last enjoyed a rejuvenation of its economic fortunes under the occupation of the French and the Prussians. Fundamental changes were to lead to rapid reform. Dissolution of church property and eventual abolition of the guilds; the recognition of both religious and commercial freedom; the legal equality of all citizens; and the creation of a uniform German domestic market all helped clear the way for Cologne's resurgence. The sale of secularized church land to investment-hungry entrepreneurs from the beginning of the 19th century also contributed to the expanding number of new businesses.

The rise of the industrial revolution also promoted the rapid growth of small suburbs, such as Ehrenfeld, Deutz, Kalk, and Mülheim, and these areas eventually expanded to become towns in their own right. Cologne's connection to the rapidly growing rail network in the 1840s and 1850s added further momentum. Completion of the Hohenzollern Bridge in 1859 made Cologne a transport hub connecting all points of the compass. Among the many important industries to develop at this time were textiles, manufacturing, foodstuffs, and, from the end of the 19th century, the chemical industry.

Such rapid economic expansion led to the growth of population and a subsequent need for further housing. Following tough negotiations with the Prussian military authorities, in 1881 Cologne purchased the inner defensive ring, a semi-circular wall around the city. This 104-hectare (half-a-square-mile) site was to be developed using modern methods to the designs of the Aachen town planners Henrici and Stübben. Copying Parisian town planning and the Viennese ring road, Cologne's street plan was laid out with arterial roads and side streets, central squares, and a magnificent boulevard as a ring road. Various dormitory suburbs were laid out beyond the ring road, with imposing residences and mansions. The workers' quarters were sited next to the St Gereon and Bonntor goods stations and near the slaughterhouse at Ehrenfeld.

Above left: Houses in Cologne were numbered during the "French period". A certain perfumery in the Glockengasse received the number 4711, which later became the brand of the world-famous "Original Eau de Cologne". Above right: The Hohenzollern Bridge is embellished with statues of Prussian kings on horseback, an expression of power typical for the period.

Completion of the cathedral

The most visible indication of Cologne's growth and prosperity in the 19th century was the completion of its Gothic cathedral. With the decline in fortune and reputation of the medieval Hanse towns, construction work on it had stopped in the 16th century through lack of funds. In the ensuing three hundred years, the cathedral's masons had concentrated on repairs and renovation of the chancel, nave, transept, and aisle. It was not until the early 1800s that the German architect Sulpiz Boisserée, an outspoken critic of Napoleon and an admirer of the cathedral, begged the Prussian king, Frederick William IV, to renew work on it. Thirty years were to pass before building recommenced, not least because the matter of costs had to be settled between the Prussian state and the city of Cologne. Eventually, however, a decision was reached to share the burden equally, and in 1842 Frederick William IV authorized the work, personally laying the foundation stone on 4 September. Completion of the cathedral was to be carried out as prescribed by what plans remained from the medieval masons, but executed according to modern methods. Within a few decades both the north and south spires had

Progress and history: when the iron framework over the choir in the cathedral was built, it was considered the most modern roof construction in the world.

grown to 157 m (515 feet), the height from which they survey the town to this day. (For a few years the cathedral was the highest building in the world.) On 15 October 1880, after 600 years of

Top: Artisans removing the spire tips.
Above: Kaiser Wilhelm I at the inauguration in 1880.

construction work, the completion of the cathedral was solemnly celebrated in the presence of the emperor, William I. It was declared a UNESCO World Heritage Site in 1996.

From left: The city center in 1945; the Old Town, with the destroyed Hohenzollern Bridge in the background and the cathedral, which had been hit by 14 bombs and partially destroyed. Cologne's Old Town lay almost completely in ruins and all of today's alleys and streets are reconstructions. There are very few old houses remaining in the heart of the city.

December 1918
English troops occupy Cologne. Mayor Konrad Adenauer cooperates with Sir Charles Fergusson, the military governor.

20 June 1919
Official inauguration of the university in the Gürzenich. Mayor Adenauer receives an honorary doctorate.

11 May 1924
Opening of the first spring trade fair in Cologne.

29 October 1926
Westdeutscher Rundfunk broadcasting moves to Cologne.

28 February 1928
First Rose Monday procession through Cologne since the beginning of World War I.

3 March 1933
Clashes between Communists and National Socialists in the Elsassstrasse.

13 March 1933
Local Nazi leader Grohé announces that Adenauer has been deposed.

April 1937
Adolf Hitler authorizes the expansion of Cologne as a regional capital.

9 November 1938
Three synagogues are burnt down in Kristallnacht (Night of Broken Glass).

28/29 June 1943
Devastating Allied carpet-bombing of the city.

Konrad Adenauer

A former city councillor and a future federal chancellor, Konrad Adenauer was elected Mayor of Cologne in 1917, remaining the city's highest official until 1933. Certain achievements will always be associated with his term of office: the university, which had been closed by the French, was reopened in 1919, the trade fair was established in 1924, and a greenbelt was created both inside and outside the city. Adenauer succeeded in tempting the Hamburg civil engineer Fritz Schumacher from the Elbe to the Rhine for three years, between 1920 and 1923. Schumacher drew up plans to convert land won back from the defortification of Cologne into two areas of greenery, pleasing the nature-loving mayor. The inner greenbelt was intended as a bridge between the densely built-up Old Town and city center and the suburbs; the outer greenbelt provided a natural border between the town and its surroundings. Along with town planning, Adenauer was also concerned with Cologne's commercial and cultural regeneration after World War I and was instrumental in the re-establishment of the university in 1919; Cologne had never been able to come to terms with the Prussian decision to seat the university of the Rhine in Bonn.

To promote Cologne's commerce and manufacturing, Adenauer also militated for the re-opening of the trade fair and in 1922 the council acceded to the mayor's wishes, earmarking a sum of 152 million marks for the reconstruction of the trade fair halls. This was carried out on the banks of the Rhine at Deutz and the building was opened in 1924, in the presence of the president, Frederick Ebert, and the chancellor, William Marx.

Solid as Rhine rock: Konrad Adenauer.

The nights of bombing

In contrast to many German cities, Cologne was an early target of Allied bombing raids in World War II; night operations, flown by the RAF to target residential areas, were particularly devastating. Carpet-bombing was carried out according to an established set of principles: airborne mines and high explosives first destroyed the roofs and these were followed by incendiaries intended to ignite the flammable contents of the houses. A last wave of high explosives was intended to delay firefighters. After such a raid on 3 November 1943, the cathedral looked ready to collapse; this was narrowly prevented by sappers and forced labourers plugging the hole that had been blown in the wall with 27,500 bricks, the so-called "cathedral filling".

As the battle front drew nearer to Cologne, the city suffered its worst raids in 1944 and 1945, and by the time the Americans arrived on 6 March 1945, the city lay in ruins. In 262 recorded air raids, 20,000 people had died, with a further 50,000 injured. The majority of the survivors had fled the city or had been forcibly evacuated. The northern and southern parts of the Old Town lost 87 percent and 93 percent of their buildings respectively. The suburbs on the right bank of the Rhine were also badly affected, especially the industrial areas of Kalk, Deutz, and Mülheim.

From top: World War I veterans at a Nazi rally in 1936; terror measures against the Jews continued even during the bombing: a Cologne Jew's stamped identity papers; Hitler in Cologne in 1939.
Right: View across the destroyed Hohenzollern Bridge to the cathedral.

From left: Recent examples of Cologne's rich cultural life include personalities like the actor Willy Millowitsch (shown here in 1974); writer and Nobel Prize-winner Heinrich Böll (1966); composers Karlheinz Stockhausen (1995) and Hans Werner Henze (2004); artist Gerhard Richter (2002); publishers Alfred Neven DuMont and Alice Schwarzer; and rock musician Wolfgang Niedecken.

1946
First local elections after the war; the CDU was initially the strongest party, then the SPD from 1956–1994. The mayors were all SPD until 1999.

1948
The first Taunus (the "humpback Taunus") rolls off the production line in the Ford works in Niehl.

1957
Opening of W. Riphahn's Opera House; first new building of its kind in Germany after 1945.

1966
The Zoo Bridge becomes the last Rhine Bridge to be completed to date.

1972
Heinrich Böll (1917–1985) receives the Nobel Prize for Literature and the freedom of the city.

1985
Completion of restoration work on the twelve Romanesque churches.

1986
Opening of the Museum Ludwig and the Cologne Philharmonic, next to the cathedral.

January 1995
The second "flood of the century" (after December 1993) sees the Old Town submerged by water.

2005
The newly elected Pope Benedict XVI celebrates World Youth Day on the Marienfeld meadow among hundreds and thousands of the faithful.

Cologne as an industrial town

Only a few companies continue to have a strong presence within industrial Cologne in the 21st century, and first among these are the Ford works in Niehl. Founded in 1930, this branch of the American concern has survived all the economic highs and lows of the post-industrial world, and with more than

Top: Photokina. Above: Ford car plant.

20,000 workers is now one of the region's largest employers. The end product manufactured in Cologne is the Fiesta, for which components are transported to the Rhine from all over Europe. Numerous smaller suppliers in the immediate area of the car plant ensure that the vehicles are assembled "just in time".

A metropolis of millions

With about a million inhabitants spread over 40,515 hectares (156 square miles), Cologne is Germany's fourth-largest city. It is the only city on the Rhine with a population of a million or more, and its importance now resides less in its administrative and political influence and increasingly in its economic might and its artistic and cultural role. Today the service industry has the largest turnover in Cologne, employing four-fifths of the total workforce.

After World War II, the debris left behind had to be cleared away and reconstruction undertaken so the inhabitants could return to live in Cologne and it could regain its former glory. A city was created, not necessarily more beautiful than the old one but certainly more modern and better suited to the ever-increasing motor traffic that began rolling out of the Ford works in Niehl once more in 1948. Ring and arterial roads like the north-south link road, new bridges including the Zoo Bridge (1966), the Rhine Tunnel (1982), multi-storey car parks, and a metro system (from 1968) all helped the city adapt to the demands of an era on the move. Cologne-Bonn airport and the central station with its ICE (international express) connections all link Cologne with the outside world.

The rebuilding of Cologne was not just a matter of introducing new architecture, as instanced by the WDR television building on the Wallrafplatz (1952) and W. Riphahn's Opera House (1957); old traditions had to be restored and revived as well. The tiny houses of the Old

Town lying at the foot of the cathedral were thus rebuilt to their original dimensions and today form a link between the Rhine jetties and the Hohe Strasse, a gateway for the four million tourists a year who visit the city.

Even if you won't find the real Lindenstrasse (from the German television drama serial) in Lindenthal, Cologne has every right to call itself a media city: 10 percent of the

The old and avant-garde: the cathedral and Museum Ludwig.

The Kölnarena, opened in 1998.

WDR galleries.

workforce is employed in communications, a third of all German television output is produced in the local studios, and eleven broadcasters, including Westdeutscher Rundfunk, are based in this metropolis on the Rhine.

Peter Ludwig

Peter Ludwig and his wife have joined a long line of great collectors, patrons, and supporters of the arts which includes Ferdinand Franz Wallraf, Alexander Schnütgen, Johann Heinrich Richartz, and Josef Haubrich, who have found fertile ground for their passion in Cologne. In 1951 Ludwig, a history of art graduate born in Koblenz in 1925, found in Irene Monheim a partner who would share his interests and who now administers their joint bequest as a trust after her husband's death in 1992. The money needed for this "professional hobby" was made by Ludwig in his wife's chocolate-making business. In 1957 the Ludwigs began to

Peter Ludwig, art collector.

feature on the Cologne and Aachen museum scene and in 1976 they donated 300 works, particularly of Russian avant-garde and pop art, to the city of Cologne for the first Museum Ludwig. The second museum of this name, a spectacular new build located between the cathedral chancel and the gardens on the Rhine, was constructed between 1980 and 1986. Nowadays the Ludwig collection is shared between 19 museums and art institutes in five countries.

The Cologne Tower in the MediaPark, a media industry hub.

COLOGNE CATHEDRAL
RONCALLIPLATZ

The heart of Cologne is to be found in front of the cathedral. Past and present meet here, in the square Roncalliplatz: it is a meeting place for locals and tourists alike, and the echo of ancient history is as routine as the throb of the modern, while art and culture are represented by the Museum Ludwig and the Römish-Germanisches Museum. Above all this towers the cathedral, one of the largest Christian buildings and guardian of the relics of the Three Kings: a destination for pilgrims from around the world.

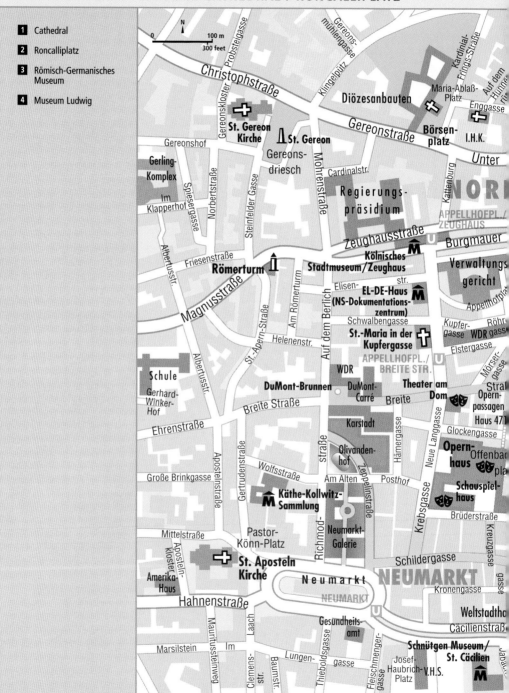

1 Cathedral

2 Roncalliplatz

3 Römisch-Germanisches Museum

4 Museum Ludwig

N
0   100 m
300 feet

Gereons-mühlengasse

Probsteigasse

Gereonskloster

Christophstraße

Klingelpütz

Kardinal-Frings-Straße

Maria-Ablaß-Platz

Auf dem Hunne...

Enggasse

Diözesanbauten

Gereonstraße

Börsen-platz

I.H.K.

St. Gereon Kirche

St. Gereon

Gereonshof

Gereons-driesch

Cardinalstr.

Unter

Gerling-Komplex

Norbertstraße

Steinfelder Gasse

Mohrenstraße

Kattenburg

NOR...

Im Klapperhof

Spiesergasse

Regierungs-präsidium

APPELLHOFPL./ZEUGHAUS

Albertusstr.

Friesenstraße

Zeughausstraße

Burgmauer

Römerturm

Am Römerturm

Kölnisches Stadtmuseum/Zeughaus

Verwaltungs-gericht

Magnusstraße

Elisen-str.

EL-DE-Haus (NS-Dokumentations-zentrum)

Appellhofpl...

St.-Apern-Straße

Helenenstr.

Auf dem Berlich

Schwalbengasse

St.-Maria in der Kupfergasse

Kupfer-gasse WDR gasse

Elstergasse

Albertusstr.

Schule

Gerhard-Winker-Hof

WDR

APPELLHOFPL./BREITE STR.

Mörser-gasse

DuMont-Brunnen

DuMont-Carré

Breite

Theater am Dom

Stral
Opern-passagen

Ehrenstraße

Breite Straße

Karstadt

Hämergasse

Neue Langgasse

Glockengasse

Haus 471

Große Brinkgasse

Aposteinstraße

Gertrudenstraße

Wolfsstraße

straße

Olivanden-hof

Am Alten

Posthof

Zeppelinstraße

Krebsgasse

Opern-haus

Offenbac...pla...

Schauspiel-haus

Käthe-Kollwitz-Sammlung

Brüderstraße

Kreuzgasse

Mittelstraße

Aposteln-kloster

Pastor-Könn-Platz

Richmod-

Neumarkt-Galerie

Schildergasse

gasse

Amerika-Haus

St. Aposteln Kirche

Neumarkt

NEUMARKT

Kronengasse

Hahnenstraße

Mauritussteinweg

Laach

Im

NEUMARKT

Weltstadth...

Cäcilienstraß...

Marsilstein

Clemens-str.

Baumstr.

Lungen-gasse

Thieboldsgasse

Fleischmenger-gasse

Gesundheits-amt

Schnütgen Museum/St. Cäcilien

Josef-Haubrich-Platz

V.H.S.

Jabau...

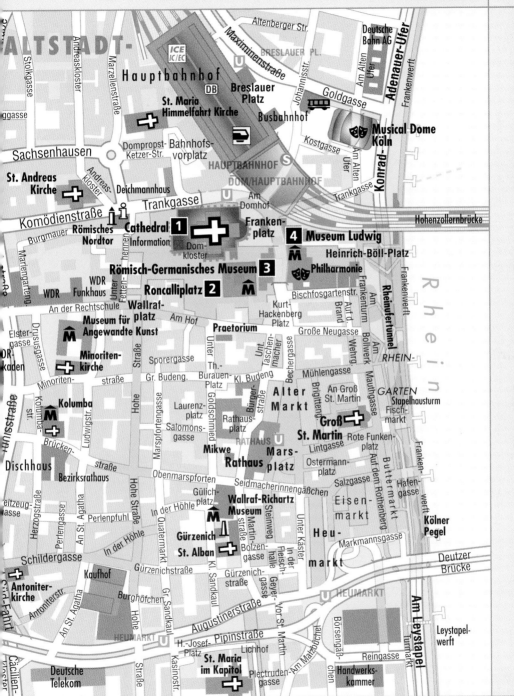

ALTSTADT-

Stolkgasse

Andreaskloster

Marzellenstraße

Altenberger Str.

Maximinenstraße

BRESLAUER PL.

Deutsche
Bahn AG

Johannisstr.

Am Alten Ufer

Adenauer-Ufer

Frankenwerft

ICE
IC/EC

Hauptbahnhof

DB

St. Maria
Himmelfahrt Kirche

Breslauer
Platz

Goldgasse

Busbahnhof

Musical Dome
Köln

ggasse

Sachsenhausen

Dompropst-
Ketzer-Str.

Bahnhofs-
vorplatz

Kostgasse

Am Alten Ufer

Konrad-

St. Andreas
Kirche

Andreas
kloster

Deichmannhaus

HAUPTBAHNHOF

Am
Domhof

Trankgasse

DOM/HAUPTBAHNHOF

Trankgasse

Hohenzollernbrücke

Komödienstraße

Burgmauer

Römisches
Nordtor

Cathedral 1

Information

Dom-
kloster

Franken-
platz

4 Museum Ludwig

Heinrich-Böll-Platz

Mariengarten

Römisch-Germanisches Museum 3

Philharmonie

WDR

WDR
Funkhaus

Roncalliplatz 2

Bischfosgartenstr.

Rhein

Wallraf-
platz

Am Hof

Kurt-
Hackenberg
Platz

Rheinufertunnel

Museum für
Angewandte Kunst

Praetorium

Große Neugasse

RHEIN-

Elster-
gasse

Drususgasse

Minoriten-
kirche

Sporergasse

Unt. Taschen-
macher

Bechergasse

Mühlengasse

Bolwerk

GARTEN

Stapelhausturm
Fisch-
markt

OR-
kaden

Minoriten-
straße

Th.-
Gr. Budeng.

Burauen-
Platz

Kl. Budeng.

Brigitteng.

An Groß
St. Martin

Mautgasse

Kolumba

Hohe

Laurenz-
platz

Goldschmied

Alter
Markt

Groß
St. Martin

Rote Funken-
platz

Brücken-
straße

Ludwigstr.

Marspfortengasse

Salomons-
gasse

Rathaus-
platz

RATHAUS

Lintgasse

Auf dem Rothenberg

Dischhaus

Bezirksrathaus

Obenmarspforten

Mikwe
Rathaus

Mars-
platz

Ostermann-
platz

Salzgasse

Hafen-
gasse

eitzeug-
gasse

Herzogstraße

Perlengasse

An St. Agatha

Perlenpfuhl

Hohe Straße

In der Höhle

Gülich-
platz

Seidmacherinnengäßchen

Eisen-
markt

Kölner
Pegel

Schildergasse

Kaufhof

Quatermarkt

In der Höhle

Wallraf-Richartz
Museum

Steinweg

Martinstraße

Unter Käster

In der
Fleischhalle

Heu-

Markmannsgasse

Deutzer
Brücke

Antoniter-
kirche

Antoniterstr.

An St. Agatha

Burghöfchen

Gr. Sandkaul

Gürzenich

St. Alban

Bolzen-
gasse

Gürzenich-
straße

Geyer-Vor St. Martin

markt

Cäcilien-
kloster

Schildergasse

Kaufhof

Augustinerstraße

H.-Josef-
Platz

Pipinstraße

Lichhof

Am Marzbüchel

Börsengäß-
chen

Börsengäß-
chen

HEUMARKT

Am Leystapel

Turmstr.

Deutsche
Telekom

Straße

Kasinostr.

St. Maria
im Kapitol

Plectruden-
gasse

Handwerks-
kammer

Reingasse

Leystapel-
werft

INFO Cologne Cathedral

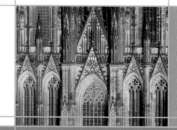

The largest Gothic cathedral in the world, begun in 1248, is the heart of "Holy Cologne".

Domkloster 4; 6.00–19.30 daily (no sightseeing during services); U-/S-Bahn Dom Hbf.

Below from left: The magnificent house of God, seen from the east; the splendid south façade and portal; the art of the mason in the service of God. Below inset: The knocker on St Peter's Door; temporal power, immortalized in stone.

The mighty size of the cathedral is only hinted at by the impressive 4-m (12-foot) long original plan of its west façade. With its two spires and 7,000 sq. m (75,000 square feet) of stonework, this is the cathedral's public face. To the right of the central entrance is the Petersportal (St Peter's Door). Of the twelve doorways into the cathedral, it was the only one to receive five of its statues in the Middle Ages, including those of the brother Apostles Andrew and Peter (unfortunately, this 14th-century statuary has since had to be replaced with copies). The portals in the south façade have a modern treatment: the mighty bronze doors were begun by the sculptor Ewald Mataré only in 1947. The corner of the west and north façades long bore a scar from World War II: a buttress had been patched up with bricks in 1944, and the 823 carved blocks of sandstone that were needed to restore it to its former dignity only became available in 2005.

THE HIGHLIGHTS:
COLOGNE CATHEDRAL

INFO Climbing the spire

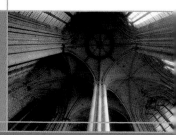

The viewing platform is a sweat-inducing 509 steps high, past the world's largest swinging bell.

Below: Fine tracery in a window; breathtaking verticality; a vaulted aisle roof. Right: Magical light effects, which change with the time of day, thanks to the stained glass.

Nov–Feb 9.00–16.00, daily, Mar–Apr, Oct 9.00–17.00, daily, May–Sep 9.00–18.00, daily.

THE NAVES AND CHANCEL

The chancel of the cathedral carries almost 700 years of history: it was consecrated in 1322, 74 years after the foundation stone was laid. The 14th-century choir stalls seat 104 people and are the largest in Germany. The construction of the naves reflects the ups and downs of the cathedral's history: only fragments of them had been completed by the 16th century, when building work was stopped for 300 years. Today the ceiling of the central nave curves some 43 m (143 feet) above the heads of visitors; the aisles are almost 20 m (66 feet) high.

In good weather, light floods into the cathedral through 10,000 sq. m (108,000 square feet) of glass, and the detailing of the figures at the foot of the pillars in the central nave is clearly visible. They are impressive examples of carving dating from the 19th century onwards.

The verticality of Gothic architecture symbolizes a striving for heaven, a point made particularly strikingly by the first glimpse of the 43-m (143-foot) high central nave of Cologne Cathedral (below left). The large image (middle) was taken during the Papal celebrations of the cathedral's 750th anniversary in 1998. The image below right is of the chancel, looking east. Right: The intricate architecture of the cathedral's east façade and the high, vaulted roof of the central nave.

GOTHIC ARCHITECTURE

The term 'Gothic' was initially intended pejoratively. Art and architecture from the period was looked down upon as if it had been the work of the supposedly barbaric Goths, and yet it was a style that opened up new dimensions from the Romanesque period that it succeeded. Gothic art had its roots in 12th-century France, but within a century it had spread throughout Western Europe. Churches were constructed according to the latest principles of civil engineering: vaulted ceilings were lent stability with ribs, the weight of the building was diverted to external buttresses, pointed arches could carry more weight than rounded ones. Tracery windows became a typical feature, their glass reinforced and separated by slender stone supports. Gothic churches also characteristically had two spires, and the first building to follow this model was Magdeburg Cathedral, begun in 1209. Its Cologne counterpart, begun in 1248, had an even more sophisticated form. The buildings became ever more refined, the masons ever bolder in the brinkmanship of their designs. Sometimes they went too far: Beauvais Cathedral in France, for example, partially collapsed in 1284.

In the 13th century, the new self-assurance among the citizenry found expression in public buildings in the Gothic style such as town and guildhalls; Cologne's best-known example of this is the Gürzenich.

Below: A detail from the front of the 2.2-m (7-foot) long Shrine of the Three Kings, with the Adoration of the Magi on the left and the Baptism of Christ on the right. This treasure is to be found behind the High Altar (inset, left). The Gero Crucifix was revered by the faithful in the building preceding the current cathedral (right).

The cathedral's treasure is to be found in a 13th-century vault: reliquaries and liturgical apparatus, as well as the insignia of the Archbishop of Cologne.

Tel. (02 21) 17 94 05 30; 10.00–18.00, daily.

Cologne Cathedral's architecture is impressive enough, but the art historical and religious significance of the church is further enhanced by two treasures within. Hanging on the wall of its dedicated chapel, the famed Gero Crucifix, a larger than life depiction of the crucified Christ carved from oak in the 10th century, is the oldest surviving large medieval sculpture in central and northern Europe. More famous still is the 1.5-m (5-foot) tall Shrine of the Three Kings. Built at some point after the end of the 12th century, this is the largest reliquary to survive from the Middle Ages and is one of the most impressive achievements of the goldsmith's art of the period. It is said to house the remains of the biblical Three Kings, who are especially honored on their saint's day, 6 January. The relics were brought from Constantinople to Milan in the 4th century, and from there to Cologne in 1164.

The 15th-century altarpiece of the Three Kings is Stephan Lochner's masterpiece and one of the cathedral's treasures (small images top and below). The Altar of the Poor Clares is about 100 years older and its intricate carving is of similar art historical significance.

Even when closed, Stephan Lochner's Altar of the Three Kings of 1442 is monumentally large: the two wings are 3 m (10 feet) across and 2.6 m (9 feet) high. When opened, the altar is twice as wide, revealing the great artist's depiction of the Annunciation in all its delicacy, tenderness, and magic. In the central panel, the Three Kings worship an enthroned Madonna and Child. Surrounding the group is a multitude of followers. The Altar of the Poor Clares, which is painted on the outside and carved on the inside, is both older than Stephan Lochner's piece and larger still. Finished around 1350, its pair of double wings fold out to a width of more than 6 m (20 feet). The wings are unfolded only on special holy and feast days, revealing the delicate carved sculptures of a group of twelve Apostles, which are 55 cm (22 inches) tall. Restoration of the altar began in 1970 and took twelve years of painstaking work.

Stephan Lochner worked for at least a decade in Cologne. *The Last Judgement* was originally located in the Laurentius Church and can be seen today in the Wallraf-Richartz Museum (right). Below from top: The artist has immortalized himself in the Altar of the Three Kings in the cathedral; the central figure of the altar is Mary with the baby Jesus; a similar motif is to be found in the painting of the *Madonna of the Violets* in the Wallraf-Richartz Museum.

STEPHAN LOCHNER

Anyone wanting to see Stephan Lochner's *oeuvre* will have to travel: the works of the late Gothic master are to be found as far afield as Darmstadt, Frankfurt, Nuremburg, Munich, and Lisbon. However, Cologne Cathedral houses the most famous example of Lochner's great art: St Maria's Chapel is home to the tripartite Altar of the Three Kings, once admired by Albrecht Dürer and lauded by Heinrich Heine. Stephan Lochner was born *circa* 1400 in South Germany. By 1442, at the latest, he had arrived in Cologne via Flanders, and was to die in the city around 1451. He is the best-known member of the Cologne school of artists and, significantly, brought the individual to the foreground. He often portrayed his subjects with idealized faces typical of the Gothic period, yet he also made many realistic portraits. Lochner generally avoided perspective in his backgrounds, preferring expanses of gold as expressions of the divine. This is exemplified in the Altar of the Three Kings, which has as its focus Mary with the Christ child on her lap. Lochner's work is also exhibited in two museums in the city: the *Madonna of the Violets* which hangs in the Kolumba Museum was only rediscovered in the 19th century, having been overpainted, and the *Madonna in the Rose Bower* in the Wallraf-Richartz Museum was chosen as a design for a Christmas stamp in 2005 – a true sign of popularity.

The cathedral workshop is the workplace of numerous masons and glass restorers (right and below right), led by Barbara Schock-Werner (inset below). Below: Plaster casts used as a starting point for restoration work.

CATHEDRAL WORKSHOP

A building as old and as large as the cathedral is never really finished. Sections of façade have to be restored, eroded sculptures must be replaced and the roofs must be continually kept in order; the 60 artisans of the Cathedral Workshop are responsible for all of this. There was a time when the "cathedral building site" was an exclusively male preserve, but that is now long past; the workshop has been led by a female master mason since 1999. The artisans work in the same tradition as that observed in the first workshop of 1248. When the cathedral, which had been left incomplete into the 19th century, was finally finished, up to 500 men were simultaneously employed.

Today, masons and sculptors make up the bulk of the workforce, supported by a team of roofers, joiners, and painters. Ten restorers and glaziers are responsible for the windows alone, and two precious-metal workers look after the treasures inside.

Just how laborious the work of cathedral maintenance can be is demonstrated by the historic lead roof, 80 percent of which was destroyed in World War II. Although it was initially patched up with zinc, which was replaced piecemeal with lead, within a matter of decades the whole structure had become so fragile that a complete restoration had to be started in 1985. It took a further eleven years before the new roof shone out above the city.

THE HIGHLIGHTS:
RONCALLIPLATZ

Roncalliplatz is at the heart of Cologne's festivities, whether it be for the Christmas market or the World Youth Day in 2005 (inset, below left). When the crowds have gone, the square is left free for the skateboarders (below). Eye-catching pavement art directly in front of the cathedral (below right).

TIP Domhotel

A great view of the cathedral, excellent food and drink, and a sun terrace: a place that fulfils its promise.

Domkloster 2a; Tel. (02 21) 202 40; restaurant 6.30–23.00, daily; U-/S-Bahn Dom Hbf.

If a city could be said to have a lounge, then Roncalliplatz is Cologne's lounge. The cathedral lies to the north, the Römish-Germanisches Museum is between the square and the Rhine. The central station is nearby and the shops on the Hohe Strasse and Schildergasse are but a few paces away.

Summer in particular transforms the square into a stage for those free spirits who make art both their life and their living: young people on skateboards swerve competently round the crowds of tourists, pavement artists present their work for admiration, jugglers, buskers, and mime artists all find an audience here, and children love simply splashing about in the fountain.

Large stages regularly host exclusive concerts by Cologne bands, or even international stars, and no one could want for entertainment in winter at the traditional Christmas market.

THE HIGHLIGHTS:
RÖMISCH-GERMANISCHES MUSEUM

INFO Römisch-Germ. Museum

The Römisch-Germanisches Museum has housed a wealth of treasures from Cologne's ancient past for over three decades, and here visitors can admire Lucius Poblicius' monumental tomb (below). A collection of rather more modest gravestones (right).

Discover a comprehensive and informative presentation of the early part of the city's 2,000 years of history. The collection of Roman glassware, one of the largest in the world, is particularly recommended. *Roncalliplatz 4; Tel. (02 21) 22 12 44 38; Tues–Sun 10.00–17.00; U-/S-Bahn Dom Hbf.*

In 1941 an astonishing discovery brought excavation work for an air-raid shelter to a halt. At the workers' feet lay a 3rd-century Roman mosaic, composed of 1.5 million tiles, which was to become as famous as the Dionysus Mosaic. Some years later, the Römisch-Germanisches Museum was built on the site of the discovery, opening in 1974. The museum houses other outstanding Roman antiquities, including the tomb of Lucius Poblicius, which was discovered beneath Cologne in 1967, and towers some 40 m (132 feet) high. For those unable to face a tour of the whole collection, both of these treasures can be viewed from outside through large glass windows, but the museum offers much more. Nowhere on earth is there as much Roman glassware as here, and an arch from a Roman gate engraved with the letters CCAA is a reminder of the city's original name: Colonia Claudia Ara Agrippinensium (see p. 178).

Visitors to Cologne who are looking for the Romans are often obliged to go underground. This drainage tunnel (below) belongs to the Praetorium, the seat of the Roman governor. A section of the aqueduct, which once brought water into the city from the Eifel region, can be seen in the Luxemburger Strasse (below right). Remains of a bath underneath Gross St Martin and remains beneath St Severin's (right); a grave chamber a little further out of the city (inset left); part of the Hafenstrasse, the Roman docks road (inset right).

ROMAN HERITAGE

A stroll through the city quickly reveals the legacy of the Romans. The Praetorium is a good starting-point. Situated where the Town Hall stands today, in the 1st century this was the residence of the proconsul, governor of the Roman province of Germania Inferior. The underground remains of the palace can still be viewed today. The most important Roman remains above ground are individual remnants of the city wall. Tourists love to photograph one another in front of the side entrance of the cathedral's north portal, but a stone's throw from here, in the underground car park, there are still sections of the wall to be found. The largest surviving section – 140 m (450 feet) of the original 2 km (2.5 miles) – is a little out of the way in the city, in the Mauritiussteinweg. Unfortunately, traces of only two of the original nineteen towers of the city's mighty defences remain today. The best preserved of these is the Römerturm (Roman Tower) at the north-west corner of the ancient city. Its crenellations are nothing to do with the Romans, however; they were added only a century ago, when such "historical" touches were fashionable. One particular Roman relic cannot be reached on foot by daytrippers: it is a grave chamber on the Aachener Strasse, which was once part of an estate. Climb down into the 12-sq-m (130-square-foot) crypt and marvel at the perfectly preserved carved sarcophagus.

INFO Museum Ludwig

The new Museum Ludwig was architecturally impressive on the inside as well as the outside (inset, right). Gerhard Richter's *Ema, Nude on a Staircase* is part of the permanent collection. In 2006 an exhibition was devoted to Salvador Dali (below).

Features modern art from the 20th century, including internationally famous masterpieces and any number of paintings by Picasso.

Heinrich-Böll-Platz; Tel. (02 21) 22 12 61 65; Tues–Sun 10.00–18.00, every first Fri of the month 10.00–22.00; U-/S-Bahn Dom Hbf.

Only the galleries of Paris and Barcelona have more works by Pablo Picasso than the Museum Ludwig. Its collection of several hundred pictures by the master painter was created by Peter and Irene Ludwig, who collected modern art for decades. From the 1970s on they donated it to the city, sometimes as a gift, sometimes on permanent loan. Their only stipulation was that an appropriate gallery be built. When the astonishing, galvanized building, located between the cathedral and the Rhine, opened in 1986 it caused a furore. The Wallraf-Richartz Museum was also housed here until 2001; since then 20th- and 21st-century art has become the focus of the collection. The Museum Ludwig holds works by artists as disparate as Andy Warhol, Salvador Dali, and Joseph Beuy: a temple to modern art in the shadow of the cathedral (see p. 182).

Musicians of every era and style have been associated with the city of Cologne. The composers Max Bruch and Jacques Offenbach were born here in the 19th century, Karl-Heinz Stockhausen taught at the school of music until his death at the end of 2007, and Wolfgang Niedecken founded the cult Kölsch rock band BAP (inset images top, from left). Below: The underground Philharmonie concert hall and the Musical Dome.

COLOGNE, CITY OF MUSIC

Street names like Spielmanns-gasse ("busker's street") would suggest that Cologne was a hub for music as early as the Middle Ages. The Gürzenich, the famous ballroom and assembly room, has hosted festivities since the 15th century, and at some point after that the famous Gürzenich Orchestra was founded, with whom composers such as Wagner, Verdi, and Brahms appeared in the 19th century. In 1986 the newly opened Cologne Philharmonie (Concert Hall) became the new home of both the Gürzenich Orchestra and the WDR Radio Symphony Orchestra. Not far from the Philharmonie, the blue glass and steel construction of the Cologne Musical Dome has been attracting music enthusiasts from all over Germany since 1996. As a result Cologne has become a home for music from all eras and in all styles, from classical through the noises from the Westdeutscher Rundfunk radiotronics workshop to songs by groups singing in local dialect, like Bläck Fööss und Höhner. In Germany, however, BAP is the name is most associated with Cologne; Wolfgang Niedecken's band made so-called "Kölsch rock" famous throughout the country.

The renowned Hochschule für Musik (University of Music) is devoted to the music of the future, teaching contemporary and dance music, as well as jazz. For many years, Karl-Heinz Stockhausen and Mauricio Kagel, the acclaimed avant-gardist composers, both taught at the university.

THE HIGHLIGHTS

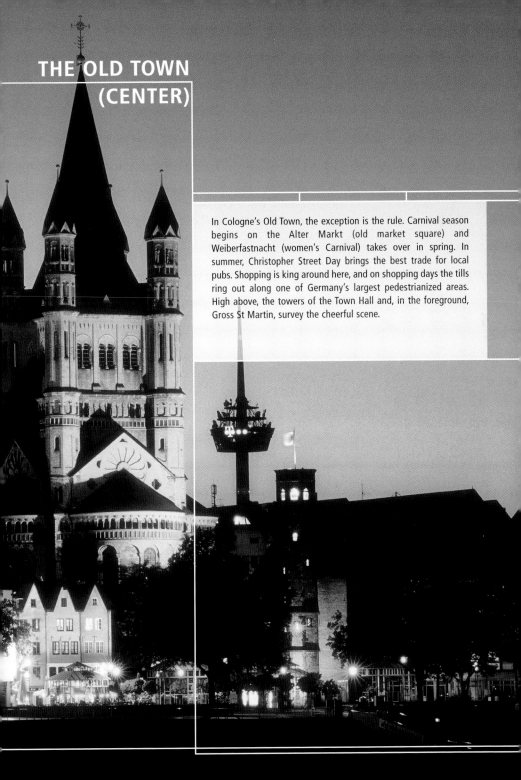

THE OLD TOWN (CENTER)

In Cologne's Old Town, the exception is the rule. Carnival season begins on the Alter Markt (old market square) and Weiberfastnacht (women's Carnival) takes over in spring. In summer, Christopher Street Day brings the best trade for local pubs. Shopping is king around here, and on shopping days the tills ring out along one of Germany's largest pedestrianized areas. High above, the towers of the Town Hall and, in the foreground, Gross St Martin, survey the cheerful scene.

5 Town Hall

6 Alter Markt, Heumarkt

7 Gross St Martin

8 Wallraf-Richartz-Museum

9 Hohe Strasse, Schildergasse, Neumarkt

10 St Aposteln

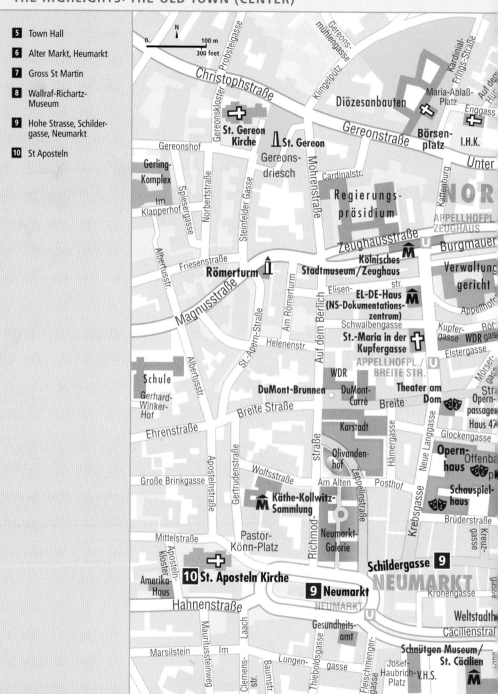

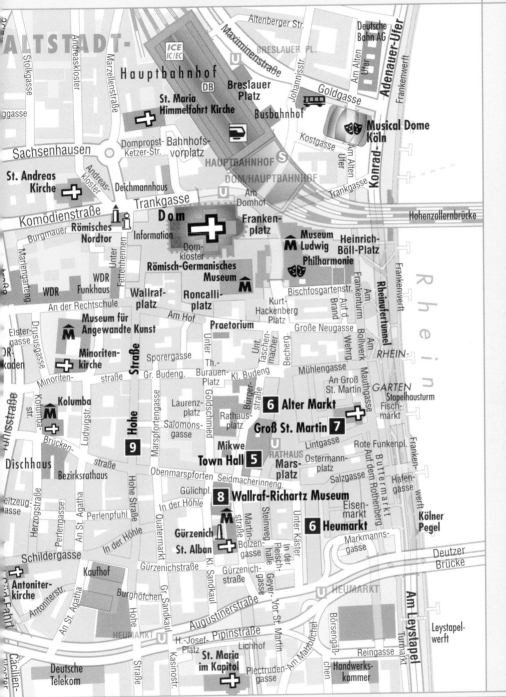

ALTSTADT-

Hauptbahnhof

ICE IC/EC

Altenberger Str.

Maximinenstraße

BRESLAUER PL.

Deutsche Bahn AG

Adenauer-Ufer

Am Alten Ufer

Frankenwerft

Stolkgasse

Andreaskloster

Marzellenstraße

DB

St. Maria Himmelfahrt Kirche

Breslauer Platz

Johannisstr.

Goldgasse

ggasse

Busbahnhof

Kostgasse

Musical Dome Köln

Sachsenhausen

Dompropst-Ketzer-Str.

Bahnhofs-vorplatz

Am Alten Ufer

Konrad-

St. Andreas Kirche

Andreas-Kloster

Deichmannhaus

HAUPTBAHNHOF

Trankgasse

S

DOM/HAUPTBAHNHOF

Am Domhof

Trankgasse

Hohenzollernbrücke

Komödienstraße

Dom

Frankenplatz

Burgmauer

Römisches Nordtor

Information

Museum Ludwig

Heinrich-Böll-Platz

Unter Fettenhennen

Dom-kloster

M

Philharmonie

Frankenturm

Rheinufertunnel

Rhein

Mariengarten

WDR Funkhaus

Römisch-Germanisches Museum

Bischofsgartenstr.

Am Bollwerk

WDR

An der Rechtschule

Wallraf-platz

Roncalli-platz

M

Kurt-Hackenberg Platz

Auf dem Brand

RHEIN-

Elster-gasse

Drususgasse

Museum für Angewandte Kunst

Am Hof

Große Neugasse

Am Wehrg.

GARTEN

Straße

M

Praetorium

Unter

Unt. Taschen-macher

Becherg.

Mauthaus

Stapelhausturm Fisch-markt

Minoriten-kirche

Sporergasse

Th.-Burauen-Platz

Kl. Budeng.

Mühlengasse

An Groß St. Martin

Minoriten-straße

Gr. Budeng.

Burger-

6 Alter Markt

Hohe

straße

Laurenz-platz

Goldschmied

Rathaus-platz

7 Groß St. Martin

Rote Funkenpl.

Auf dem Rothenberg

Franken-werft

Kolumba

Kolumba-str.

Ludwigstr.

Salomons-gasse

Mikwe

Lintgasse

Ostermann-platz

Butter-markt

Hafen-gasse

Brücken-

Hohe Straße

Town Hall 5

RATHAUS

Mars-platz

Salzgasse

Kölner Pegel

Dischhaus

Bezirksrathaus

Obenmarspforten

Seidmacherinneng.

9

Gülichpl.

In der Höhle

8 Wallraf-Richartz Museum

Eisen-markt

Deutzer Brücke

eitzeug-asse

Herzogstraße

An St. Agatha

Perlenpfuhl

M

6 Heumarkt

Markmanns-gasse

Schildergasse

In der Höhle

Gürzenich

St. Alban

Steinweg

Bolzen-gasse

Gürzenich-straße

In der Fleisch-halle

Geyer-Vor St. Martin

Am Leystapel

Antoniter-kirche

Antoniterstr.

An St. Agatha

Kaufhof

Burghöfchen

Gr. Sandkaul

Kl. Sandkaul

Gürzenich-straße

U HEUMARKT

Börsengäßchen

Turmarkt

Leystapel-werft

Cäcilien-

Deutsche Telekom

HEUMARKT U

Augustinerstraße

Hohe

H.-Josef-Platz

Pipinstraße

Kasinostr.

Lichhof

St. Maria im Kapitol

Plectruden-gasse

Am Malzbüch-

Reingasse

Handwerks-kammer

THE HIGHLIGHTS:
THE OLD TOWN (CENTER)

TIP Keule

Below: The entrance to the Prophet's Chamber, leading to the tower and the Senate Room beneath it. The walls of the Hansasaal are decorated with eight 15th-century sculptures of the prophets (below right). Right: A view of the Town Hall tower and the Renaissance loggia at the front of the building.

A good solid cafe with a long bar, plenty of Kölsch, and a hearty, rustic style of cuisine.

Heumarkt 56–58; Tel. (02 21) 258 11 59; Mon–Tues 11.00–1.00, Fri–Sat 11.00–3.00, Sun 11.00–23.00; U-Bahn Heumarkt.

Cologne Town Hall is the oldest in Germany, but, like so many other buildings here, it did not escape the devastation of Word War II and what we see today is a partial restoration. The heart of the building dates back to the 14th century and has been continually expanded. The eye-catching Renaissance-style loggia was added in the 16th century. Also of note is the Hansasaal, the room in which the members of the Hanse declared war on the Danish king Waldemar in 1367. The 61-m (200-foot) tall late Gothic tower dominating the Town Hall had to be rebuilt after World War II. Until recently it was decorated with 124 stone sculptures representing people who had played a part in Cologne's history, among them Konrad Adenauer and Heinrich Böll. Since the statues had weathered badly, they were removed to safety.

THE HIGHLIGHTS:
THE OLD TOWN (CENTER)

An atmosphere of medieval-tinged romanticism with plenty of tourist traffic: the bars and cafés in the lanes between the Alter Markt and the Heumarkt are a popular meeting place.

TIP Gaffel-Haus

A listed building housing a tavern with a comfortable medieval feel; fine food and beer are on tap.

Alter Markt 20–22; Tel. (02 21) 257 76 92; 11.00–1.00, daily; U-Bahn Heumarkt.

Any tour of the Old Town begins at the Alter Markt, the old market. The Jan von Werth fountain and the 16th-century houses are a delight for the eye. The square is of vital importance in November, as Carnival begins here on the eleventh day of the eleventh month at 11.11. In the middle of the Old Town, it's easy to forget that the hubs of the Roman and medieval towns lay elsewhere. There are bars, souvenir shops, and flea markets to attract the tourists, and the Rhine and Gross St Martin are only a few steps away.

Anything but enchanting, the Heumarkt to the south has retained few of its original features and what little history that remains is dominated by a modern hotel building. The Deutz Bridge round the corner confirms that here the car is king.

Although the Carnival is a lot of work for the maiden, the prince, and the farmer, it is not of the worst kind. Constantly waving as they sit in state at numerous occasions, they are always rubbing shoulders with the public (below), and are never alone, even during the procession, when the prince's guard and honor guard put in an appearance (right).

THE PRINCE AND HIS HONOR GUARD

Many a Cologne resident has dreamt "Einmol Prinz zu sin, in Kölle am Rhing..." ("Just once to be a prince in Cologne on the Rhine..."). The Prinz, Bauer, and Jungfrau (the prince, farmer, and maiden) have been the three most important figures in the Karneval (Cologne Carnival) for 200 years. As the first official Rose Monday procession wove its way through the heart of the city in 1823, the prince, accompanied by "His Ribaldness" the farmer, was still known as the "Carnival Hero" and embodied the Romantic idea of the merry prince. Even today he bears a shield and a coat of arms to represent the city's defensive capabilities, and the farmer is equipped with the keys to the city, a shirt of chain mail, and a flail. The maiden is the third of the triumvirate, for beneath her costume and wig there always lurks a man. "Her Loveliness" is a symbol of the independence of the city of Cologne and her creneflated crown represents the unbroached medieval city wall. A different club every year is responsible for providing this carnival "trefoil". Carnival season means hard work for these three gentlemen; between their enthronement by the mayor at the beginning of the year and Ash Wednesday they make about 400 public appearances. Since the early 20th century, the farmer and the maiden have been accompanied by the "guard of honor"; the prince has his own personal retinue, the "prince's guard", and thus arrayed they represent Cologne Carnival, ready for any foolishness.

Below middle: A brief pause in festivities. Right: Women's Carnival is the beginning of the street Carnival. Inset below left: the brighter the costume, the better. Inset below right: The Rose Monday procession tempts hundreds of thousands of revellers out onto the streets.

WOMEN'S CARNIVAL, ROSE MONDAY

Woe betide any man daring to wear a tie in public on the day of Women's Carnival; once the women have taken control, every tie they come across is symbolically snipped off with their scissors. The street Carnival is officially open from eleven minutes past eleven on the dot, and the 10,000 revellers assembled on the Alter Markt begin to drink and sway to the festive music. After this extensive open-air session, celebrations continue into the small hours in every pub and bar in the city.

The absolute highpoint of the "fifth season" comes on Rose Monday (before Ash Wednesday), as the procession winds its way for over 7 km (4.5 miles) through the city and 10,000 participants – on horseback, on foot, or transported on one of the giant floats – greet the public with a slogan that changes every year. Some 130 bands provide the musical backing and an audience of up to a million people waits for hours along the procession route to welcome the floats of the various great carnival clubs. Dutiful shouts of "Strüüsscher" and "Kamelle" from the public are greeted with a shower of bouquets and no less than 140 tons of sweets.

At the end of the procession the public is rewarded with the sight of the prince, the farmer, and the maiden accompanied by their respective guards.

THE HIGHLIGHTS:
THE OLD TOWN (CENTER)

Gross St Martin is a symphony of Romanesque arches and pillars. A simple icon is displayed on a side altar (below right). Among Gross St Martin's other treasures is a triptych created in 1530, depicting the Adoration of the Magi (below inset, right).

TIP Haxenhaus

You'll find homemade Bratwurst (sausages) and hearty Haxen (legs of pork) prepared in every way imaginable, as well as daily menus, specials, and tasting menus.

Frankenwerft 19; Tel. (02 21) 947 24 00; Sat–Thurs 11.30–1.00, Fri 11.30–3.00; U-Bahn Heumarkt.

If any of Cologne's Romanesque churches deserves its name, it is Gross St Martin (St Martin's the Great); it has dominated the city's skyline since its completion in 1250, when building work on the cathedral, now much higher, had barely begun. Its mighty quatrefoil tower has a smaller tower at each corner and this unique feature has become almost a trademark. The people of Cologne were horrified in 1942 when the church roof burnt down, and in 1945, at the very end of World War II, an air raid destroyed the tower and large portions of the building. The symbolic importance of the reconstruction work on the tower, completed in 1965, cannot be overstated; it was another twenty years before the whole church was restored to its former magnificence. Inside the church, a few painted fragments dating from the 19th century were all that could be saved from the destruction.

A "Stammtisch" (regulars' table, below middle) is unthinkable in Cologne without Kölsch. The "Köbes" replaces empty "Stangen" with full ones carried in a special container (below left). The brew bars are popular with locals and visitors alike. Beer gardens are often laid out outside the bars, such as at the Volksgarten (right). Visitors to the Heller and Päffgen breweries get to look behind the scenes, seeing for example the mash tun and barrel-filling (below, far right).

KÖLSCH: BREWING IN COLOGNE

Visitors to a Cologne brewery are not only plied with food and drink; they also receive a tutorial in the particulars of "Kölsch". Often brewed on the premises, this is drunk not from a normal glass but from a so-called "Stange", a little beaker holding only a fifth of a litre (7 fluid ounces). This soon is finished but fortunately the waiter, invariably called the "Köbes", needs no prompting to bring a replacement; anyone deciding they have had enough need only place their beer mat on top of the glass. Caution is advised: if you don't want to be ignored all evening by the waiter, don't order mineral water. The menu in a traditional brewery bar is every bit as simple as the bare tables and décor; having ordered a "Halve Hahn", which sounds like it ought to be a chicken dish, many a tourist has been surprised to receive instead an open rye roll with cheese. "Himmel und Ääd" ("heaven and earth") is potato puree with apple sauce and fried blood sausage; other tavern favorites include "Riev-koche" (potato fritters) and "Hämche" (pork knuckle). Brewing Kölsch (the name is protected by law) dates back to the 14th century and is as natural a part of Cologne culture as the cathedral. There are six large brew bars in the Old Town, and breweries are also to be found in the southern suburbs as well as the Friesian Quarter.

If asked to name a Cologne character, most Germans would think of Willy Millowitsch. A past master of folk theater, he was on stage almost until his death in 1999. He is shown below in the play *The Spanish Fly*. Millowitsch was so popular in his home town that in 1992 a statue was erected in his honor in the Eisenmarkt (below left). Another monument in the Old Town is dedicated to the Cologne characters Tünnes and Schäl, as realized by Wolfgang Wallner (right).

COLOGNE CHARACTERS

Tünnes and Schäl, the two figures who most perfectly embody typical Cologne characteristics, sadly never actually existed in real life. Tünnes, the Rhine nickname for Anton, is a loyal, rustic, down-to-earth character with a big nose and red hair. Schäl, tall and with a squint, is cunning and scheming. The character of Tünnes has existed since at least 1803 as a member of the puppet ensemble at the Hänneschen Theater in Cologne, and Schäl was created in the middle of the 19th century by the puppet master Franz Millewitsch as a sly attack on the theater director of the time. The puppet master could little have suspected that one of his descendants, Willy Millowitsch, would later find fame as Cologne's most celebrated personality of the 20th century. As manager, principal lead, and director of his own theater, Willy Millowitsch became a legend, and a statue was erected in his honor in the Eisenmarkt (Iron Market) while he was still alive. His many films and countless television appearances, including his last role as Inspector Klefisch, made him famous throughout Germany. Trude Herr, an actress with quirky Cologne manners, also found a fame that reached far beyond the city walls. She was known as "Dat Pummel" and, before her death in 1991, she led a theater troupe in the south of the city; the premises are now used as a cinema.

INFO Wallraf-Richartz-Museum

An outstanding collection of art from the 13th to the 20th century housed in a building by the German architect Oswald Mathias Ungers.

Obenmarspforten; Tel. (02 21) 22 12 11 19; Tues, Wed, Fri 10.00–18.00, Thurs 10.00–22.00, Sat, Sun 11.00–18.00; U-Bahn to Heumarkt.

Cleverly placed windows link the inside and outside world in the gallery (below and inset, left). The treasures range from medieval altars to modern sculpture (below right). The gallery moved to its current location in 2001 (right).

The Wallraf-Richartz Museum belongs among the top rank of German art galleries. It has long specialized in showing paintings from the Middle Ages to the 19th century, featuring artists such as Stephan Lochner and Albrecht Dürer, as well as Rubens, Rembrandt van Rijn, and François Boucher. The oldest gallery in Cologne, its original premises were paid for by Johann Heinrich Richartz while the nucleus of the collection was amassed by Ferdinand Franz Wallraf. After several changes of address, including a short interregnum when it shared a location with the Museum Ludwig, the collection moved into its cube-like new home in 2001. Its focus shifted too: with the acquisition of Gérard Corboud's collection of impressionist paintings as a permanent loan, the gallery was officially rechristened the Wallraf-Richartz Museum – Fondation Corboud (see p. 180).

The Hohe Strasse is known for being the most popular shopping strip in the Cologne pedestrianized zone (below). The Weltstadthaus department store, boldly designed by Renzo Piano, has a magnificent glass façade (right).

TIP Neumarkt Passage

A busy mall with many shops, restaurants, and even culture; it is home to two internationally renowned institutions, the Käthe Kollwitz Museum and the Lew Kopelew Forum.

Neumarkt; U-Bahn to Neumarkt.

If you follow the main streets of the pedestrianized zone, you walk in the footsteps of the Romans. The Hohe Strasse was the ancient city's main north-south link, which was crossed from east to west by the Schildergasse. The streets were given their current layout during the reconstruction work following World War II. The narrow Hohe Strasse was turned into one of Germany's first pedestrianized zones and the broader Schildergasse, leading to the Neumarkt, a central square in the city, became one of the country's most popular shopping streets. All the big chain stores have branches either here or in the pedestrianized zone, and the square, which is surrounded by roaring traffic, is an inner city hub for ten tramlines.

The middle of the square is reserved for special events such as demonstrations, visiting circuses, and the traditional Christmas Market.

Below, from left: Tilman van der Burch completed his *Christ as the Man of Sorrows* in 1500. The chancel of St Aposteln displays a certain rigor in its form. The ceilings were painted in the later 20th century by Hermann Gottfried. The *Pietà*, although not medieval, does not look out of place here.

TIP Diner's

A comfortable cross between a snackbar and a bistro. Just right for a quick bite to tide you over. A generally good selection, whether for breakfast or lunch, coffee and cake, or supper.
Neumarkt 16; Mon–Fri 6.00–22.00, Sat 6.00–18.00, Sun 12.00–17.00; U-Bahn to Neumarkt.

There is one fixed point that stands among the office buildings and the roaring traffic around the Neumarkt: the church of St Aposteln, whose 65-m (215-foot) high west tower is a beacon amid the worldly bustle. Capped with a distinctive octagonal dome, the tower is also eight-sided, as are both towers on the east side of the building.

The clover-leaf-shaped chancel of this Romanesque church is also notable as an example of the successful integration of ancient and modern art forms. After the reconstruction work that followed World War II, three apses as well as the barrel-vault ceiling were left undecorated. The repainting work was not started until 1988 and was finally completed in 1994, with the finished pieces harmonizing successfully with their medieval Romanesque setting.

The original 4711 house number is still proudly displayed as a trademark in the home of "Eau de Cologne" (below). The advertising has changed, but the product is the same; the images (right) show advertisements from 1928, 1939, and 1959. Gables above, arcades beneath – the company headquarters in the Glockengasse has striking architecture. The shop windows are decorated not just with 4711 bottles but also with a whole range of products bearing the number (below, from left).

EAU DE COLOGNE

One of the most famous numbers in the world is 4711, although initially it was nothing more remarkable than a house number. When Wilhelm Muelhens and Catharina Moers married in 1792, a Carthusian monk gave them a recipe for a "miraculous liquid", and Muelhens subsequently founded a company in the Glockengasse to mass-produce this concoction. Shortly afterwards, the French occupied Cologne and in an attempt to make getting around the city less challenging they gave each house a number for ease of identification. Muelhens's house received the number 4711 and this soon became famous as the trademark of his "Eau de Cologne". High society ordered the product and the Muelhens family were appointed court suppliers to the French royal family. By the end of the 20th century the brand was well established worldwide, and the family firm sold the business to a large cosmetics concern, which in turn was taken over by an American multinational. In 2006 the rights were acquired by a firm from Aachen; thus, now only the name remains from its Cologne heritage.

Nevertheless, the modern Glockengasse is no less proud of its history. The original building was rebuilt after World War II in a Neo-Gothic style, creating a fairytale appearance, which is reinforced by the carillon that plays hourly from 9.00 until 19.00.

THE HIGHLIGHTS

THE OLD TOWN (NORTH)

The Hauptbahnhof (central station) dominates the northern part of the Old Town. Built 150 years ago and at first sight seemingly out of all proportion with the buildings around it, the station is now seamlessly integrated into a cityscape that includes the adjoining Hohenzollern Bridge, and what was once seen as a disruptive intrusion has long since become an emblem of the city. Three of Cologne's twelve Romanesque churches lend the area described in this chapter a historic feel: St Gereon, St Ursula, and the northernmost, St Kunibert.

11 Hauptbahnhof, Hohenzollern Bridge

12 St Kunibert

13 St Ursula

14 St Gereon

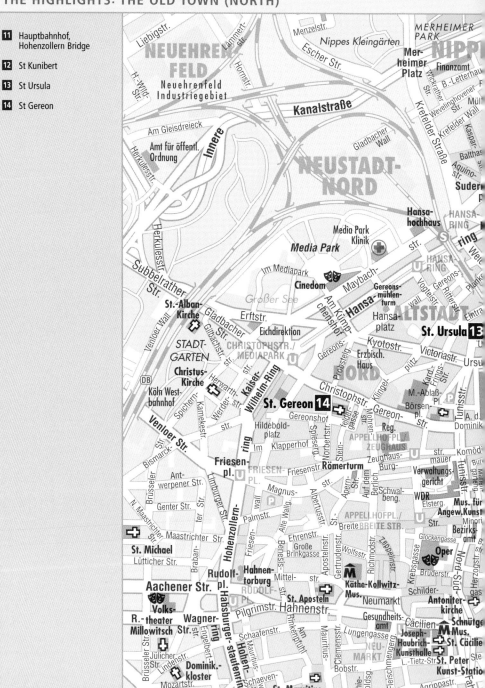

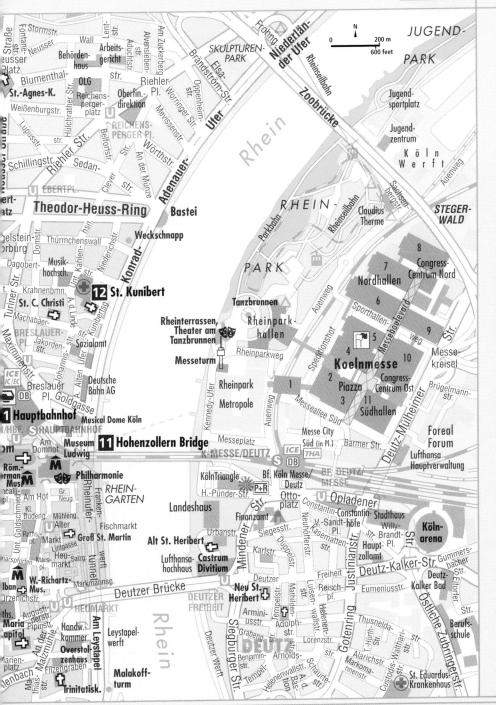

THE HIGHLIGHTS:
THE OLD TOWN (NORTH)

Along with the view of the Hohenzollern Bridge, no cityscape of Cologne is complete without the cathedral, the emblem of the city (below). The new roofs make even the rear of the station worth seeing (right). More than a thousand trains stop in the main hall every day (inset below).

TIP Alter Wartesaal

In the Old Waiting Room beneath the station, you can enjoy modern German and Mediterranean cuisine in art nouveau surroundings. An ideal place to meet for a Kölsch after going to the Philharmonie. *Johannisstr. 11; Tel. (02 21) 912 88 50; 18.00–1.00, daily, Sun also 10.30–15.00; U-/S-Bahn Dom Hbf.*

It is rare to arrive by train as close to the heart of a city as in Cologne. The first thing the visitor sees on arrival in the station is the cathedral, and directly behind that the pedestrianized zone. Cologne was first connected to the rail network in 1839, and in 1850 the site of the old botanical gardens was sacrificed to allow work to begin on the station. Today, the steel and glass exterior of the arrivals hall in Germany's largest interchange station is a reminder of the great industrial age of the 19th century; its interior, however, has long been adapted to modern requirements.

The Hohenzollern Bridge was opened by Emperor William II in 1911. Destroyed by bombs during World War II, it was initially restored and then widened at the end of the 1980s. It now serves the needs not only of the railway, but also of pedestrians wishing to enjoy a view of the cathedral.

The pillars direct the gaze up to the vaulted roof (below middle). Among the interior's most important pieces are the figures of the Gothic proclamation group from 1439 (below left and right); St Kunibert and the television tower (right); two exquisite motifs in the Romanesque windows (inset below).

TIP Oyster

New international cuisine with ingredients fresh from the market; the menu changes daily. Emperor Frederick III, father of William II, dined in this historic house in the 19th century.
Thürmchenswall 62; Tel. (02 21) 992 32 71; Mon–Sat 17.00–1.00; U-Bahn Ebertplatz.

St Kunibert, a late Hohenstaufen vaulted basilica with three aisles, is the youngest of Cologne's twelve Romanesque churches. It was consecrated in 1247, before the building was finished and a year prior to work beginning on the cathedral, when Gothic was the newest architectural fashion. Finally completed only in 1992, after all kinds of architectural compromises, St Kunibert was also the last church of the dozens destroyed in the bombing raids during World War II to be restored. The church's interior houses numerous precious artefacts, including valuable Gothic sculptures and paintings, but one treasure is unique throughout Germany: the priceless apse windows, finished in 1230, have survived 800 years more or less unscathed. Hidden behind a tall altar, the stained-glass cycle of Biblical scenes was not destroyed, as often elsewhere, in the name of secularization and supposed progress. What a blessing!

St Ursula's 17th-century Golden Chamber is among Cologne's greatest treasures (below). Reliquaries in the form of busts are stored in the wall niches. Above these are slightly more gruesome sights: ornaments made of human bones; a view of the chancel to the east (right).

TIP Schreckenskammer

Don't be put off by the name (Chamber of Horrors); home-brewed Kölsch and home-made cooking await!

Ursulagartenstr. 11-15; Tel. (02 21) 13 25 81; Mon–Fri 11.00–13.45, 16.30–22.30, Sat 11.00–14.00, 17.00–21.30; U-/S-Bahn Hansaring.

Do not let the baroque cupola from 1608 lead you to believe that St Ursula is anything other than a very old church. Its origins date back to the 4th century, and its name is based on a legend: St Ursula is said to have begun a pilgrimage to Rome with ten female companions, but over the course of time a tale of eleven virgins has increased in number to a legend of an improbable 11,000. Their return journey led them to Cologne, then besieged by the Huns, and Ursula's retinue was killed. She refused to submit to the Hun leader, preferring death as a martyr. There is evidence of the storage and veneration of relics in the church's Golden Chamber from the 10th century onwards. St Ursula is a Romanesque basilica with three aisles, side-chapels, and an impressive transept to the east. The church also possesses newer, Gothic features, such as the long chancel and a second aisle to the south.

The view of the mighty twin towers awakens a suspicion that a glimpse of the decagonal interior will confirm: St Gereon is of impressive dimensions (below); the crucifixion altar in the crypt was created in 1540 (inset below).

The first bar to be open all night. A merry crowd, including locals, ordinary people, and celebrities cross the threshold here.

Friesenstr. 53; Tel. (02 21) 25 36 76; Mon–Sat from 20.00; U-Bahnen Friesenplatz.

St Gereon's cupola, built in 1227, can be compared only with that of the 6th-century Hagia Sophia in Istanbul or the 15th-century Florentine Duomo. These three are the greatest domes erected in the Middle Ages. The original building of St Gereon dates back to late antiquity and was oval in shape with eight niches. In the 13th century it was rebuilt to its current shape, a decagon. The cupola is about 34 m (110 feet) high and the deep purple paint of the interior, applied several decades ago, emphasizes the might of the architecture. The golden tongues depicted remind the faithful of the miracle of Whitsun, the descent of the Holy Spirit upon the Apostles. The church of St Gereon almost never made it to the 21st century, as a direct hit from a bomb during World War II rendered the decagon unstable; the building was not sufficiently restored to hold services until 1984.

Cologne's twelve Romanesque churches are a visual tutorial in this venerable and exciting epoch. Below from left: The view of Gross St Martin's chancel ends in three semi-circular, arched windows; the organ in St Maria im Kapitol is spanned by a semi-circular arch; looking towards the crossing in St Aposteln provides a view of the impressive vaulting. Right: St Kunibert's mighty walls were built in the time of the Hohenstaufens; the original 13th-century windows are unique.

ROMANESQUE ARCHITECTURE

Although the term Romanesque dates back only to the 19th century, the epoch whose architecture it refers to lies over 700 years before this. The most striking legacy of the period was its churches, whose innovative forms spread from France throughout the rest of Europe during the 11th century. Cologne alone has twelve magnificent examples.

Romanesque architecture draws on Roman heritage and its most typical feature is the semi-circular arch, commonly seen in the construction of windows. In contrast to basilicas of the ancient world, which occupied only a single space, churches dating from the 11th century onward developed various subdivisions, such as the nave, the transept, and the chancel. The walls and façades were lent form by relief pillars and portals, and sturdy columns were used to support the weight of the high vaulted ceilings. The churches were topped with spires, a visible representation to all of God's power.

The rapid adoption of the Romanesque style over a wide distance in Europe is the result of two sets of circumstances: clerics on pilgrimages often moved from monastery to monastery, taking new ideas with them, and masons were similarly mobile, transferring their talents from one building site to another.

THE HIGHLIGHTS

THE OLD TOWN (SOUTH)

In just a few decades the southern part of the Old Town, with its many bars and restaurants, has become one of Cologne's most popular residential areas. Impressive medieval relics are to be found around almost every corner, and St Maria im Kapitol and St Pantaleon are among the most significant Romanesque churches. However, a desire to embrace the future is unmistakable in the Rheinauhafen docks area, which has become a modern suburb. The glass shell of the Chocolate Museum and the newly glazed "crane buildings" are typical of this development.

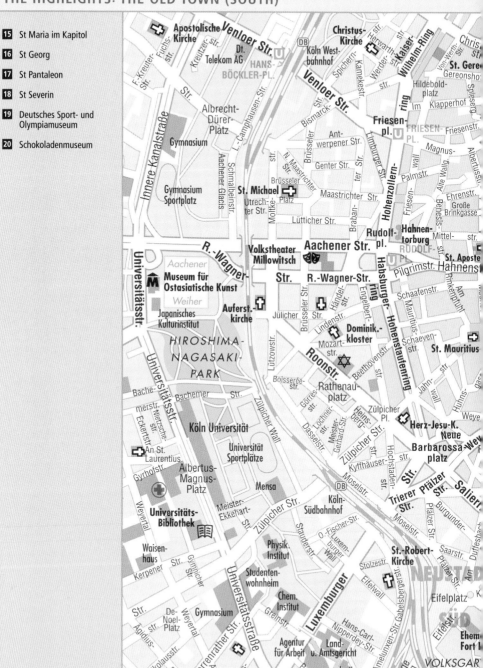

Unmistakable: the bulbous chancel of St Maria im Kapitol (below inset); the so-called "Lettner" (rood screen), built in 1525 of limestone and sandstone, separates the rear altar space from the main nave (below); view of the north conch of the trefoil chancel (below right).

TIP Malzmühle

A proper Kölsch brew bar where, as a rule, you will find lots of locals and few tourists.

Heumarkt 6; Tel. (02 21) 21 01 17; Mon–Sat 10.00–24.00, Sun 11.00–23.00; U-Bahn Heumarkt.

The bulbous trefoil ("clover leaf") chancel of the early Romanesque St Maria im Kapitol is impressive even from a distance. The church was built in the 11th century: Pope Leo IX dedicated the High Altar in 1049 and the double doors, which are among the basilica's greatest remaining treasures, were completed by 1065. Telling stories from the life of Christ, 26 scenes were carved from walnut, although four from the lowest area of the doors have been lost. No trace remains of what used to be the tallest relic of the past: the west spire collapsed in 1637 and was never rebuilt, even during the course of restoration work after World War II. Despite the missing spire, St Maria im Kapitol is a jewel in the city's twelve Romanesque churches, and at the end of the annual Romanesque Summer Festival music lovers have an opportunity to enjoy sacred music here into the hours of the early morning.

THE HIGHLIGHTS: THE OLD TOWN (SOUTH)

The 14th-century plague cross draws the eye at the western end of St Georg's (below left); the view to the east reveals the semi-circular arches of the church's architecture (middle); the windows, including this image of St Anno (right), were created by the Expressionist artist Jan Thorn-Prikker from 1928 onwards; (right) depictions of Christ.

TIP Gasthaus Schmitze-Lang

A down-to-earth tavern and cozy rendezvous for locals in the "Vringsveedel" (Severin district) with tasty, traditional cooking. The daily menu is very popular.

Severinstr. 62; Tel. (02 21) 331 84 12; Sun–Thurs 10.30–2400, Fri, Sat 10.30–1.00; U-Bahn Chlodwigplatz.

St George's Crucifix, a medieval treasure of incalculable value, used to hang in the three-aisled Romanesque church, St Georg. Today a reproduction crucifix resides in its place, and the original, dating from 1067, is stored in the Schnütgen Museum, housed in the Romanesque church of St Cecilia.

Many elements of the church are no longer original either; the building had to be laboriously restored after World War I, at which time the 16th-century entrance hall and magnificent baroque roof were still to be seen. However, these architectural treasures survived only to be destroyed during bombing raids in 1945, and they have never been rebuilt. No trace of St Georg's bright medieval interior paintwork has been retained either, yet some sense of the basilica's original solemn atmosphere is still to be felt when viewing the 13th-century font and the plague cross dating from 1380.

St Pantaleon's history stretches back to the 10th century (right). The Lettner (rood screen area, below left) was built in the late Gothic period and separates the altar from the rest of the church; above it can be seen the decorated baroque organ. The magnificent altar dates back to 1747.

TIP Weiss Bräu

A large Cologne brew bar for purists, with one peculiarity: they brew Weissbier and Schwarzbier (white and dark beer) here too. Another tip for the summer: it has a lovely roof terrace!

Am Weidenbach 24; Tel. (02 21) 23 18 23; 11.00–1.00, daily; U-Bahn Barbarossaplatz.

St Pantaleon lies in a little oasis in the middle of the town, surrounded by the greenery of the old "immunity district" (an area traditionally under the authority of a consistory court) and protected by a high wall. The original west side and nave of this Ottonian church, which was extended in the 12th century into a basilica with three aisles, represents both one of Cologne's oldest churches and the city's earliest instance of Romanesque architecture; the first abbot began his ministry in 964. Two medieval names of note are connected with St Pantaleon: Archbishop Bruno, brother of the Emperor Otto II, founded the church and Theophanu, Otto II's Byzantine wife, encouraged further building work here until her death in 991. Both are buried in the church (Theophanu's sarcophagus was completed only in 1965). The present high altar dates from 1747 and the coffered ceiling, built after World War II, was painted in 1993.

The nave of St Severin's: the old decor has been largely retained (below); a graceful Madonna from the 13th century adorns the church (below right); a cloister on the north side (below inset); at 73 m (240 feet), St Severin's is the second-tallest of Cologne's Romanesque churches (right).

TIP Haus Müller

The Haus Müller is not far from St Severin and offers a great selection of tapas, tasty fish and meat dishes, and fresh Kölsch. Nice seating outside too.

Achterstr. 2; Tel. (02 21) 9 32 10 86; Sun–Thurs 12.00–1.00, Fri, Sat 12.00–3.00; U-Bahn Severinstr.

St Severin is supposed to have died some time around AD 400, but in the south of the city Cologne's third bishop is ubiquitous: just before the Severinsstrasse ends at Severinstor (Severin's Gate) you reach Severin's Church Square, and on it is the church of St Severin. This pillared basilica and former collegiate church is the southernmost of Cologne's twelve Romanesque churches and a building has stood on this site since the 4th century. At first glance the spire may seem out of place; it is late Gothic and was built at the end of the 14th century after its predecessor had been demolished. St Severin's remains have lain in the church for centuries; an examination in 1999 confirmed that they are indeed from the 4th century. The reliquary shrine is situated in the chancel. Another reliquary, a horn, holds the remains of the martyrs Cyprian and Cornelius. Every Monday this reliquary is displayed during the "Horn Mass".

Sensual pleasure meets modern architecture: the glass panels of the Chocolate Museum in front of the Severin Bridge (below). The icon of the German chocolate brand Sarotti (below, top two images); the German Sports and Olympics Museum in Cologne is worth exploring (below, bottom two images).

TIP Schoko-Shop

Chocolate of every conceivable flavor and form is piled up here. Cologne Cathedral recreated in fine dark chocolate is irresistible.

Am Schokoladenmuseum 1a; Tel. (02 21) 931 88 80; U-Bahn Severinstr.

Anyone wishing to know what Franz Beckenbauer's football boots looked like after a long game is in the right place in the German Sports and Olympic Museum in the old customs house on the Rheinauhafen dockside: 3,000 exciting and extraordinary exhibits from the world of national, international, and Olympic sport are displayed over 2,000 sq. m (21,500 square feet) of floor space; you can admire both an original Formula One racing car and Max Schmeling's first post-War boxing licence. Sweet temptation may draw you into the adjacent Chocolate Museum, where 200 kg (440 pounds) of warm chocolate can be seen pouring from a 3-m (10-foot) high fountain. This boat-shaped glass and aluminium building takes you on a journey over three floors through the history of chocolate, and a 10-m (33-foot) high tropical greenhouse affords visitors a close-up view of cocoa, coffee, and vanilla plants.

In a few years the Rheinauhafen area by Severin Bridge (below) will have transformed itself; not only will you be able to work there, you will be able to live there too – and in modern architecture. From container terminal to an ordinary crane, the Niehl I dock offers every method of transportation and unloading (right).

THE PORT OF COLOGNE

Cologne's docks are second only to those of Duisburg on the River Ruhr in terms of turnover; however, in contrast to their competitor, Cologne's docks are not concentrated in one place. The Niehl II dock to the north specializes in the transportation of oil and gas, and hundreds of new cars from the nearby Ford works also begin their river journey here. The docks at Godorf lie far to the south, alongside the heavy industry, and specialize in liquid chemicals. Niehl I has four bays and is the most diverse of Cologne's docks. Fully laden lorries are loaded and unloaded from so-called roll-on/roll-off points and there are two container ports with a combined area of 70,000 sq. m (230,000 square feet). There are only two docks on the right bank of the Rhine, at Mülheim and Deutz. The most centrally located complex is the Rheinauhafen dock, where a 170-m (565-foot) long warehouse built at the beginning of the 20th century was immediately christened the "Siebengebirge" by locals, on account of the number of gables. Only a century later, the docks area was being transformed into a business, residential, and recreational district, for which the opening of the Chocolate Museum in 1993 was the impetus. The area was officially opened in 2007, and three new developments of the Kranhaus ("crane house") are landmarks for the site. Outwardly resembling cranes, they provide office space, luxury apartments, and cultural venues.

THE HIGHLIGHTS

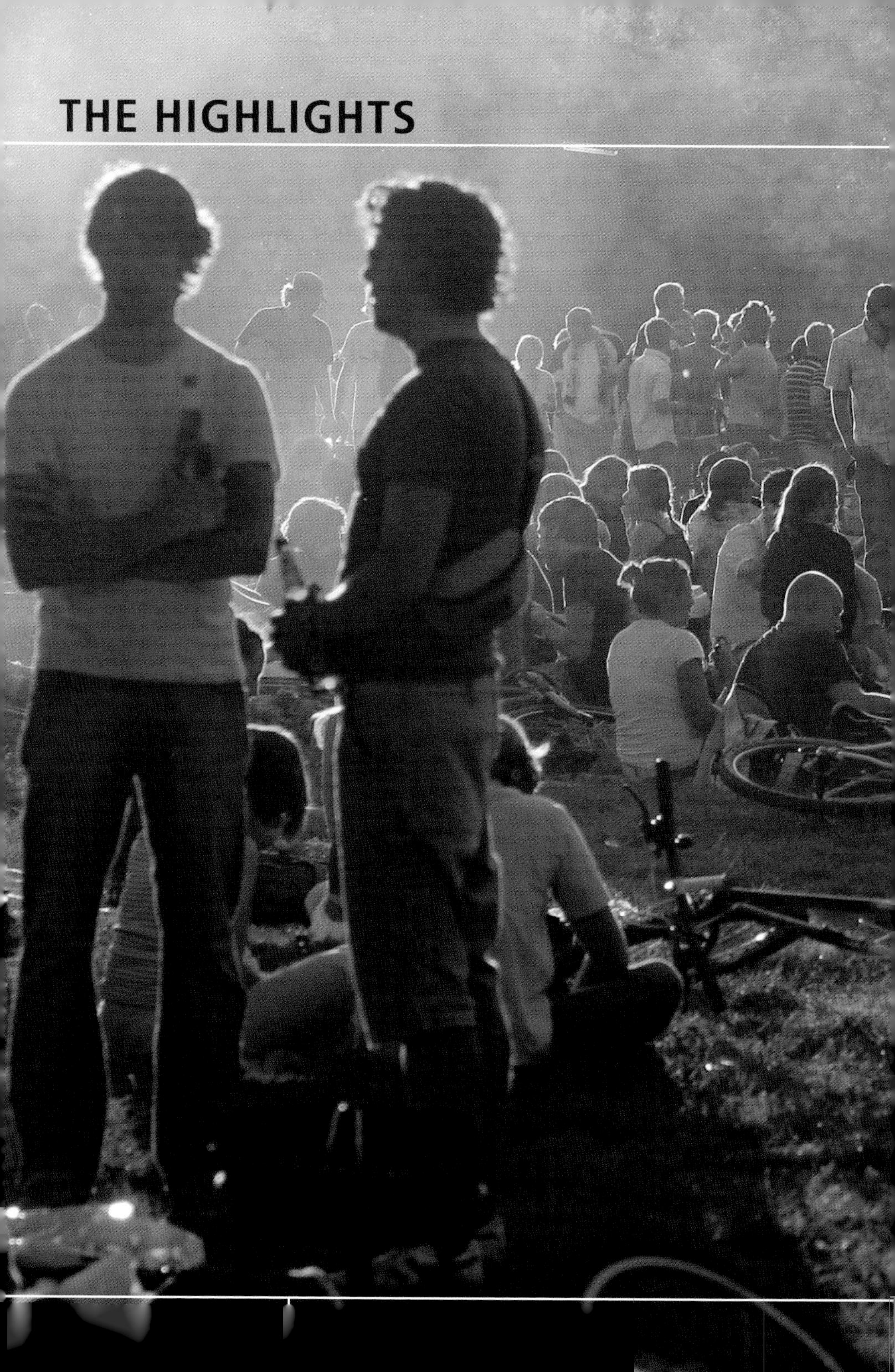

GREENBELT, THE LEFT BANK OF THE RHINE

To understand fully the qualities of Cologne, you need to see the other side of the Old Town too: there is a place of learning and scholarship, a sports venue, and an almost separate large municipal park. The university can look back on six hundred years of history and the zoo is a traditional oasis of relaxation. Even though 1. FC Cologne has seen better days, it is still one of Germany's cult teams and its ground has seen football legends come and go. The presence of the modern MediaPark is a sufficient reminder that Cologne's significance as a media hub is not to be underestimated.

21 City Wall

22 Ring Roads

23 The Zoo

24 Botanical Garden

25 Colonius Telecom Tower

26 MediaPark

27 Melaten Cemetery

28 University

29 RheinEnergie Stadium

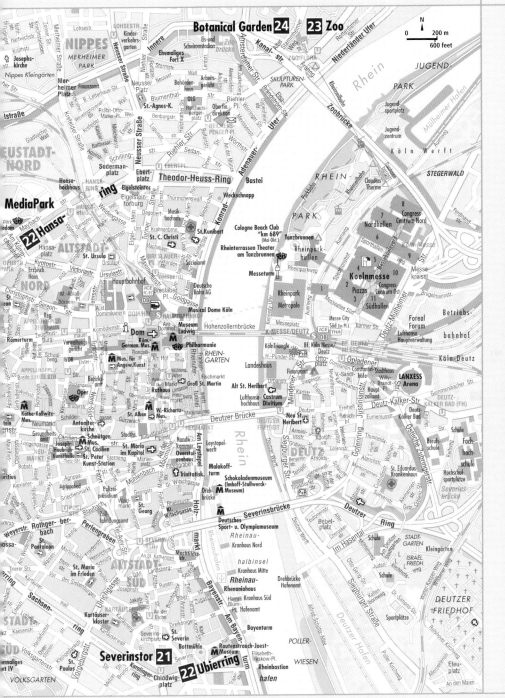

Carnival at the Severinstorburg on Chlodwig Square (below left); a brew bar in the shadow of the Severinstorburg in the south of the town (below right); the Hahnentorburg on Rudolf Square (inset, left) once protected the exit from the town towards Aachen and Jülich; the Eigelsteint Torburg in the north (inset, right).

A Kölsch brewery tap bar that has become an institution. Generous portions of home-cooked food are served here.

Chlodwigplatz 28; Tel. (02 21) 31 44 70; Mon–Sat 11.00–1.00; U-Bahn Chlodwigplatz.

Just a glance at the map reveals the semi-circular formation of the heart of Cologne. Europe's largest medieval town was surrounded by a wall. Its construction began in 1180 and when finished it was over 5 km (3 miles) long, but as ever more people flocked to Cologne during the industrial revolution and space became tight, it had to be demolished, starting in 1881. This opened the way for the wide boulevards that have become the ring roads. Nowadays they are mostly flooded with traffic, but some parts are inviting enough for a stroll. Among the most important remnants of the historic city wall are three gates, which have become emblems of the city: the Eigelsteint Torburg to the north, the central Hahnentorburg on Rudolf Square, and the Severinstorburg to the south. The Bottmühle tower in the southern suburbs is also part of the story, having been built on part of the wall in the 17th century.

Discover more than five hundred species from the world's continents and oceans in beautiful and appropriate settings.

Riehler Str. 173; summer 9.00–18.00, winter 9.00–17.00; U-Bahn Zoo/Flora.

The elephant park is the pride of the zoo and home to some twenty pachyderms; (below); inset below and far right: a few of the other zoo animals; right: the Flora's festival hall and a crown-of-thorns in the botanical gardens.

Established in 1860, the zoological gardens are Germany's third oldest after the zoos in Frankfurt and Berlin. Its format has transformed from what was originally little more than a row of cages: the 1863 elephant house is now a listed building and these days the animals live in an elephant park of some 20,000 sq. m (215,000 square feet). The tropical house is just as up to date, and has the added excitement of free-flying fruit bats. The botanical gardens, established next to the zoo in 1914, are not just given over to the exotic: there is a kitchen garden and the "Alpinum" with around 2,000 mountain plant species. The original gardens next to the cathedral had to make way for the construction of the Hauptbahnhof in the middle of the 19th century. The "Flora" arboretum was built in 1864 to exhibit a variety of tropical plants. The two institutions have long since "grown together".

THE HIGHLIGHTS:
GREENBELT, THE LEFT BANK OF THE RHINE

The Cinedom (below) was one of Germany's first multiplex cinemas. The view over the river before the film is delightful. The Colonius television tower (below right), 266 m (873 feet) high, and the KölnTurm in the MediaPark (inset below right), only 18 m (59 feet) shorter, accentuate the drama of the skyline.

TIP Mesón el Cordobés

A Spanish restaurant with a fantastic selection of fish and meat dishes. All the recipes are from southern Spain.

Gladbacher Str. 11; Tel. (02 21) 51 55 06; Mon, Tues, Thurs 11.00– 14.30 and 18.00–24.00, Sat 18.00–24.00, Sun 12.00–24.00; U-Bahn Christophstr./Mediapark.

COLONIUS TELECOM TOWER 25
MEDIAPARK 26

The Colonius Telecommunications Tower, built in 1981, might be the tallest building, but according to local wisdom the cathedral is still the greatest of Cologne's landmarks. At 266 m (873 feet) in height, the tower is taller than the cathedral by 100 m (328 feet), but its remote location in the suburb of Neustadt is not convenient for tourists and the revolving restaurant has long since closed. Neustadt is also home to the MediaPark, which offers every visitor a glimpse of the future. It was built on the site of the former Gereon freight depot. Initial construction work did not run smoothly, however: when the Cinedom opened its 14-screen multiplex in 1990, it stood almost alone on a semi-deserted site. Today the MediaPark is thriving and includes radio stations and a journalism college. The area, almost single-handedly responsible for Cologne's reputation as a media hub, is also difficult to miss: since 2001 it has been graced by the KölnTurm, a 148-m (490-foot) high office block.

The twin poles of the Cologne television world are WDR and RTL (below). WDR radio broadcasts are produced in studios on Wallraf Square (right). Facets of the media world (inset clockwise from the top): sound stages on Friesen Square; recording a television show; "Tatort" inspectors, actors Klaus J. Behrendt and Dietmar Bär; a WDR radio presenter; RTL all-rounder Günther Jauch; ARD sports round-up with Reinhold Beckmann; an RTL live broadcast; directors' conference at Stern TV; getting made up for a morning magazine show.

COLOGNE, THE MEDIA CITY

Although a few cities in Germany could lay claim to the title "media city", Cologne is considered to be the country's media hub, with over 15,000 people employed in television and radio alone; if all the freelancers in every branch of public relations are included, a total of some 50,000 people are making a living in the media sector.

Their shop window is the MediaPark, the construction of which was started in the 1990s, yet broadcasters are based throughout the city. A third of all German television is made in Cologne, for example in the studios of the Coloneum in the suburb of Ossendorf. Westdeutscher Rundfunk (WDR), Europe's largest public broadcaster, is mainly responsible for

Cologne's preeminence and its buildings are mostly concentrated west of the cathedral. The private broadcaster with the highest turnover in Europe, RTL, also has its home here on the Rhine, as does the news station n-tv. WDR leads the field in radio as well: three of its six stations are among the ten most popular in Germany. The

broadcaster Deutschlandfunk has also been of national importance for decades, and it too has its production offices in Cologne.

For the city's newspaper readers there is a choice of three local dailies, plus for the booklovers there are several large publishing houses, including DuMont and Taschen.

If Melaten Cemetery is Cologne's central point of silence and sorrow, for many in this Catholic city it is also a place of hope and redemption, as witnessed by the touching sculptures of angels on the tombs (below).

Cologne's atmospheric main cemetery has one peculiarity: wild parrots have made their homes here for decades.

Aachener Str.; Apr–Oct. 7.00–20.00, Nov–Mar 8.00–17.00; Hallowe'en/All Hallows 8.00–19.00; U-Bahn Melaten.

When Cologne's main cemetery was opened, it still lay beyond the city gates, as prescribed by hygiene regulations. From the 12th century to the 18th century, leprosy sufferers were obliged to remain here, giving the area its name; "Melaten" is derived from the French word "malade", meaning sick. Executions and witch burnings also took place here until 1797. The layout of the cemetery is indicative of the important role played by wealth even after death, especially in the 19th century. The main paths are lined with the impressive last resting places of Cologne's well-to-do citizens, whereas the less well-off had to content themselves with graves located in the second row. Many of the city's celebrities are buried here in Melaten, including the legendary folk actor Willy Millowitsch and the best-selling author Heinz G. Konsalik (*The Doctor of Stalingrad*).

Learning and swotting (below from left): a mathematics lecture and the library reading room; the pressure of tradition – a student fencing fraternity. Research (inset right): another day in the lab in the Institute of Organic Chemistry and the university teaching hospital.

A bar in the "Kwartier Lateng", as the locals call the student quarter. The central courtyard is glazed over, making a fantastic winter garden.

Roonstrasse 33; Tel. (02 21) 2 40 18 81; 17.00–1.00, daily; U-Bahn Zülpicher Platz.

Albertus Magnus still watches over the university that bears his name. A bronze statue of this 13th-century polymath guards the main building, next to the lecture theaters and the philosophy faculty. Other departments and institutes are generously distributed throughout the surrounding streets; with over 47,000 students, this is one of the largest universities in Germany. When it was founded in 1388, it was the fourth scholastic institution in the German empire, after the universities of Prague, Vienna, and Heidelberg. Dissolved during the occupation by the French in 1798, it was revived only in 1919 by Konrad Adenauer during his tenure as Mayor of Cologne and has proved resilient to this day: the Albert Magnus University has many links to international institutions and is among the most popular with students choosing first degrees.

Before the 2006 World Cup, the RheinEnergie Stadium (below) was the scene of legendary football matches under another name. Fans of 1. FC Cologne have stayed loyal to their team in every division (inset left); ever-present: cult goat and mascot Hennes VII (inset right).

More than 50,000 visitors per game can't be wrong: as far as 1. FC Cologne fans are concerned, this is Germany's most beautiful stadium.

Aachener Str. 999; Tel. (02 21) 716 16; guided tours Sat 14.00 (starting from FC Cologne Museum/north stand); U-Bahn RheinEnergie-Stadion.

In 1950 a circus donated a goat named "Hennes" to 1. FC Cologne – a reference to their player (and later manager) Hennes Weisweiler – and since then, a succession of seven generations of the mascot has been present at every home game. The team, which has produced such famous footballers as Wolfgang Overath and Lukas Podolski, has topped the German Bundesliga three times and won the cup four times. In 1975 the legendary Müngersdorf stadium was unveiled on the site of its predecessor, although a little too late to take part in the 1974 World Cup, which had been the original plan; World Cup games finally took place in the stadium, which had been rebuilt in the meantime, in 2006. The Rheinenergie Stadium, which can seat as many as 51,000 spectators, has also hosted concerts by international stars such as the Rolling Stones.

Cologne's literary scene has always had a place for both the demanding and the trivial: Heinrich Böll has always attracted much attention, and his works are compulsory reading in schools to this day (below); Heinz G. Konsalik, a master who could produce novels as if on a conveyor belt, was born in Cologne and lies buried in Melaten Cemetery (right); Dieter Wellershoff's novels and Günter Wallraff's investigative journalism were acclaimed throughout Germany (below right).

COLOGNE, CITY OF LITERATURE

When Heinrich Böll received the Nobel Prize for Literature in 1972, some of the glory was reflected on Cologne; the novels of this melancholy educator are unthinkable without the backdrop of the city's atmosphere and characters. The attention of the international literary world was once again directed here when Böll welcomed as his guests the controversial Russian authors Alexander Solzhenitsyn and Lev Kopelev, both of whom had been expelled from the Soviet Union.

Cologne has always been a good environment for creative writing: Dieter Wellershoff, Hans Werner Kettenbach, and Frank Schätzing have all found a readership beyond the city and indeed beyond the borders of Germany. The works of three women in particular have influenced the literary scene: the wry novels of Irmgard Keun, the short stories written by Elke Heidenreich, and the radical feminist Alice Schwarzer's magazine, "Emma".

The city looks after its book fans extremely well too – there are plenty of book-shops and the Literaturhaus (literature house) regularly holds readings. Spring is marked by the Lit. Cologne international literature festival, which has been attracting international authors since 2001, and the book fair later in the year offers a packed cultural programme of several days, sponsored in part by local publishers.

THE RIGHT BANK
OF THE RHINE

For many locals, Cologne proper only exists on the left bank of the Rhine; moving to the other side, the so-called "schäl Sick", would be a complete culture shock. But it is in the suburb of Deutz that Cologne's industrial pulse is particularly strong. The annual trade fair has been continually reinvented since it was established over eight centuries ago, and among the architectural highlights erected in the 21st century are the KölnTriangle skyscraper and the Kölnarena, unique in size and design.

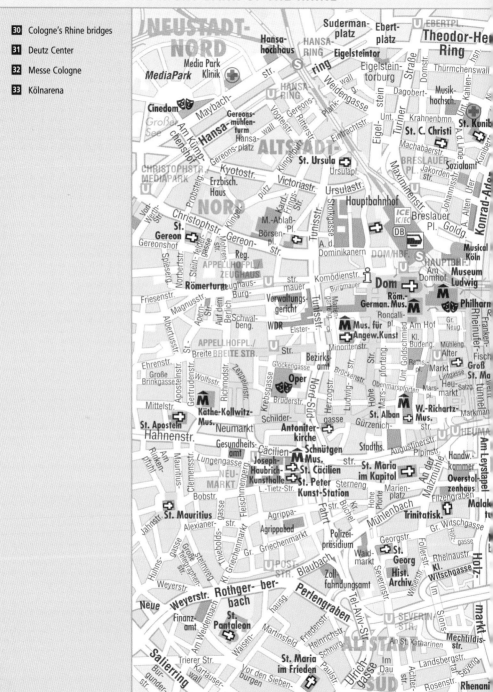

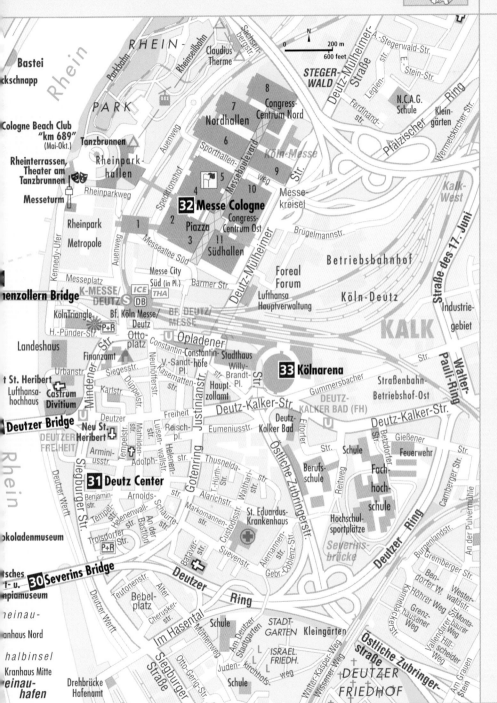

Bastei

ckschnapp

Cologne Beach Club "km 689" (Mai-Okt.)

Rheinterrassen, Theater am Tanzbrunnen

Messeturm

Rheinpark

Metropole

Messeplatz

zollern Bridge

KölnTriangle

H.-Pünder-Str.

Landeshaus

t St. Heribert

Lufthansahochhaus

Deutzer Bridge

DEUTZER FREIHEIT

koladenmuseum

sches

f- u.

piamuseum

einau-

anhaus Nord

halbinsel

Kranhaus Mitte

einau-hafen

RHEIN-

PARK

Tanzbrunnen

Rheinpark-hallen

Rheinparkweg

Parkbahn

Rheinseilbahn

Claudius Therme

Sachsen-bergstr.

Auenweg

Spethionshof

7

Nordhallen

6

Sporthallen

Messeboulevard

32 Messe Cologne

2

Piazza

3

Südhallen

4

5

10

11

Messeallee Süd

Auenweg

Messe City Süd (in Pl.)

Barmer Str.

K-MESSE/DEUTZ

ICE DB THA

Bf. Köln Messe/Deutz

BF. DEUTZ MESSE

Otto-platz

Opladener

8

Congress-Centrum Nord

Köln-Messe Str.

9

Messe-kreisel

Congress-Centrum Ost

Messe-weg

Brügelmannstr.

Betriebsbahnhof

Köln-Deutz

Foreal Forum

Lufthansa Hauptverwaltung

STEGER-WALD

Deutz-Mülheimer Straße

Legien-str.

A.-Stegerwald-Str.

E.-Stein-Str.

Ferdinand-str.

N.C.A.G. Schule

Klein-gärten

Pfälzischer Ring

Wermetskircher Str.

Kalk-West

Straße des 17. Juni

KALK

Industrie-gebiet

Finanzamt

Urbanstr.

Castrum Divitium

Deutz-Kalker-Str.

Deutz-Kalker Bad

Mindener Str.

Siegesstr.

Karlstr.

Neu St. Heribert

Arminiusstr.

31 Deutz Center

Benjamin-str.

Tempelstr.

Troisdorfer Str.

Duppelstr.

Deutzer Str.

Mathildenstr.

Freiheit

Reisch-pl.

Luisen-wall-str.

Helenenwall-str.

Helenenstr.

Adolph-str.

Arnolds-str.

An der Bastion

Schauter-str.

Batavierstr.

Neuhöferstr.

Kasematten-str.

Constantin-str.

V.-Sandt-höfe

Constantinstr.

Justinianstr.

Gotenring

Eumeniusstr.

T.-Hürth-str.

Thusnelda-str.

Alarichstr.

Markomannen-str.

Custodisstr.

Sueven-str.

Alemannen-str.

Stadthaus

Willy-Brandt-Pl.

Haupt-zollamt

33 Kölnarena

Gummersbacher Str.

DEUTZ-KALKER BAD (FH)

Eiltorfer Str.

Gießener Str.

Feuerwehr

Walther-str.

St. Eduardus-Krankenhaus

Berufs-schule

Hochschul-sportplätze

Severins-brücke

Gebr.-Coblenz-str.

Östliche Zubringerstr.

Reitweg

Betzdorfer Str.

Schule

Fach-hoch-schule

Straßenbahn-Betriebshof-Ost

Deutz-Kalker-Str.

Deutzer Ring

Walter-Pauli-Ring

Cambrer Str.

An der Pulvermühle

30 Severins Bridge

Deutzer Werft

Siegburger Str.

Bebel-platz

Teutonenstr.

Cherusker-str.

Alter Deutzer

Ring

Im Hasental

Mühlenweg

Schule

Am Deutzer Stadtgarten

Siegburger Straße

Otto-Gerig-Str.

Juden-kirchhof weg

Schule

STADT-GARTEN

L L L

ISRAEL. FRIEDH.

Kleingärten

Östliche Zubringer-straße

DEUTZER FRIEDHOF

Walter-Kasper-Weg

Wissener Weg

Burgenlandstr.

Gremberger Str.

Ben-dorfer W.

Höhrer Weg

Grenzhäusener Weg

Kannebäckerstr.

Wester-waldstr.

Montabaurer Str.

Hillscheider Weg

Vallendarer Weg

An Grauen Stein

Drehbrücke Hafenamt

Deep in the bowels of the Deutz Bridge (below): artists frequently use the pedestrian part of the tunnel for events. The 77-m (250-foot) tall Severin Bridge pylon looks futuristic against the sky (inset right, above); the 437-m (1,450-foot) long Deutz Bridge has rather simpler architecture (inset right, below).

In summer the hotel beer garden, right on the river bank, has a fantastic view of the cathedral and the Rhine. It is located at the base of the Hohenzollern Bridge on the Deutz side.
Kennedy-Ufer 2a; Tel. (02 21) 8 28 12 34; 11.00–23.00, daily; U-/S-Bahn Köln-Deutz.

Cologne's relationship with the right bank of the Rhine is complex, yet the central bridges connecting the area from the west have brought it into the heart of the city: the annual Bridge Run crosses five of them and on New Year's Eve they are all thronged with spectators wishing to see the cathedral by the light of the fireworks. The queen of Cologne's bridges is the Hohenzollern Bridge (p. 82), running close to the cathedral and affording train passengers a fantastic view as they enter the city. It is flanked to the south by two road bridges, the Deutz Bridge and the Severin Bridge; the Rhine cable car crosses the river in six minutes and runs above the Zoo Bridge to the north. There are four further bridges across the Rhine: to the north the Leverkusen and Mülheim Bridges, while at the other end of the city are the South Bridge and Rodenkirch motorway bridge.

TIP KölnTriangle Viewing Platform

The modern KölnTriangle has joined the Lufthansa building near the Deutz Bridge (below). Behind these is the illuminated pylon of the Severin Bridge (inset below). Old meets new: an equestrian statue of Wilhelm I on the Hohenzollern Bridge, with the KölnTriangle in the background (right).

From a height of 100 m (330 feet) your gaze takes in the whole city.

Ottoplatz 1; Tel. (02 21) 355 00 41 00; Oct–Apr 12.00–18.00 Mon–Fri, 10.00–18.00 Sat, Sun, public holidays, May–Sep 11.00–22.00 Mon–Fri, 10.00–22.00 Sat, Sun, public holidays; U-Bahn Deutzer Freiheit.

Only the waters of the Rhine separate Cologne's Old Town and Deutz, but they could be worlds apart. Cologne's right bank is known pejoratively as "schäl Sick", the unacceptable face of Cologne, but this is quite unjustifiable: Deutz, chartered as a town in its own right in 1888, has much to offer. For example,

the viewing platform of the KölnTriangle skyscraper, 100 m (330 feet) high, has been offering visitors a spectacular view over the city since 2005, while the "Deutzer Freiheit", which runs through the middle of Deutz, is a traditional shopping street for the residents of the right bank.

The most valuable cultural treasure is the parish church, Neu St Heribert Church, sometimes called "Deutz Cathedral", which dates back to the 19th century. In its chancel is the golden reliquary of St Heribert, finished in 1170, which complements the Romanesque treasures of Cologne's churches.

THE HIGHLIGHTS:
RIGHT BANK OF THE RHINE

TIP Deutzer Station

Urban flair: a stand at the "imm cologne" international furniture show (below). Photokina and the model railway show are among the city's most popular fairs (inset below). The north entrance to the halls and the northern conference complex (right).

Locals and trade fair delegates mingle in the old station building, with its spacious open-air terrace and cocktail bar: ideal for warm summer evenings!
Ottoplatz 7; Tel. (02 21) 880 06 15; Mon–Fri 11.00–1.00, Sat 10.00–2.00, Sun 11.00–2.00; U-/S-Bahn Köln-Deutz.

With 284,000 sq. m (70 acres) of hall space and about 100,000 sq. m (25 acres) of outside space, Cologne has the fourth-largest trade fair area in the world, which takes place directly opposite the cathedral. Its beginnings were more modest, however; the first fair was held in 1924 on a much smaller area, although this had been enlarged by 1928. Cologne's 50 international exhibitions make it a fixed point on the German trade fair scene, hosting such respected events as Photokina, Art Cologne, and the nutrition fair, Anuga. In the 1970s, the east halls were rebuilt and a venue for conferences was added. The current building consists of eleven halls; the north halls, completing this new complex, were opened only in 2006. A year previously the trade fair had given up the historic Rheinhallen halls, which have been occupied since 2008 by the television broadcaster RTL.

Art for all the senses: visitors to Art Cologne are well-fed by an Italian master chef, as shown below; children and young people too can experience modern art in the trade fair halls (below right). Expressive forms: art from Mexico and by Frank Stella from the USA (right). Art Cologne has grown ever larger over the course of four decades. Dealers, artists, and art aficionados meet up again every year (inset below).

COLOGNE AND ART

Imitators in both Basle and London have recently been trying to take Art Cologne's crown, but this successful modern and contemporary art fair will always be the oldest of its kind in the world. Begun in 1967 by two art dealers, the idea of offering works of art for sale outside a gallery environment was revolutionary, to say the least. Many gallery owners were sceptical at the time and the modest first event was held in the Gürzenich in the Old Town with no more than eighteen participants. Today, however, Art Cologne is held at the trade fair complex and participation in the ever-expanding event – in 1995 350 galleries exhibited – has had to be restricted. These days about 180 international gallery owners display their art on 55,000 sq. m (600,000 square feet) of floor space, attracting an impressive audience of 70,000 every year. The art takes on ever-different dimensions: in 2006, for example, the fair featured an installation involving twelve live horses, first realized by the Greek artist Jannis Kounellis in 1969. Held annually in spring, the Art Cologne art fair has not only made the city internationally renowned for art, but has very effectively revived the 70-strong local gallery scene. Since 2003 a fringe event, called simply "art fair", has challenged the established main event and offers artwork at affordable prices to the general public.

THE HIGHLIGHTS:
RIGHT BANK OF THE RHINE

INFO Kölnarena

The Kölnarena is the largest events venue in the country. Opened in 1998, the building looks particularly impressive when illuminated at night (below right). Handball and ice hockey matches are regularly played in the arena, and concerts by international pop stars are a highlight (below left and right).

All 18,000 seats are regularly sold out for superstar concerts and Carnival celebrations. A guided tour of the arena takes place monthly.

Willy-Brandt-Platz 1; Tel. (02 21) 80 21 (Tickets and guided tour 80 20); U-/S-Bahn Köln-Deutz.

Its 76-m (250-foot) high steel arch has made the Kölnarena (Cologne Arena) one of the most striking elements of the right bank's new skyline. The glass building, nicknamed "Henkelmännchen" ("the mess tin") by the locals because of its "handle", has 83,700 sq. m (275,000 square feet) of floor space and is the largest events venue in Germany. As the home ground of the "Sharks", Cologne's ice hockey club, it regularly welcomes 18,000 fans to cheer on their team. The Kölnarena became internationally famous at the beginning of 2007 when the German national team won the handball world championship here, captivating the nation. International rock and pop stars such as U2 and Justin Timberlake have appeared at the Kölnarena, as well as popular local bands such as Bläck Fööss and die Höhner. During the "fifth season", people drink and sing in the so-called "Laughing Kölnarena", where the city's largest Carnival celebrations are held.

Sitting on the beach in glorious sunshine, it's easy to forget that you're not at the seaside, but "merely" on the Rhine (below). House-owners living by the shore get to enjoy the view every day (right). The "Alte Liebe" restaurant is located some way from the middle of the city, but is never short of patrons (inset below).

Sun worshippers have discovered a new Eldorado, 689 km (431 miles) from the source of the Rhine. Thanks to the 300 deck chairs and 50 loungers supplied by the Cologne Beach Club on the right bank, it is now possible to sunbathe comfortably in the middle of the city. Anyone who is not inclined to visit the beach can retire to the nearby Rhine terraces and enjoy the view of the Old Town and the passing boats from the beer garden, or visit the "Alte Liebe". Now moored at Rodenkirchen in the south, the houseboat's days of travelling the Rhine are long past, but the striking red and white-painted boat is now a popular rendezvous for celebrities and people who wish to see and be seen; you can even dine there. Visitors who wish to enjoy the Rhine experience at closer quarters should take a trip on one of the pleasure cruisers; there are various ways of seeing the river, from an hour-long tour to a cruise of several days with a private cabin.

Another highlight on the Rhine is the so-called "Kölner Lichter" (Cologne Lights), usually held in July, where a convoy of 50 illuminated ships sails by night between Porz and Mülheim and some four tons of fireworks are let off: a particular highpoint of the event is a half-hour set-piece firework display with musical accompaniment which takes place on one of the boats.

AROUND COLOGNE

Many attractive places and sights await visitors beyond the city limits. The "Bergisches Land", right next door, is a delight for walkers and nature enthusiasts. There is the medieval Bergisch cathedral in Altenberg and culture vultures on the way to Bonn should stop off in Brühl to admire the country houses of Augustusburg and Falkenlust; just like the pyramids of Egypt and the Statue of Liberty in New York, these baroque gems are UNESCO-listed World Heritage Sites.

34 Altenberg Cathedral

35 Schloss Augustusburg

36 Schloss Falkenlust

37 Brauweiler Abbey

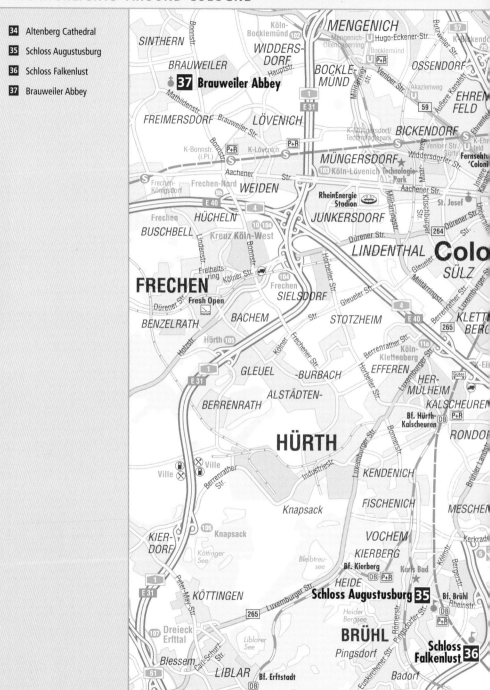

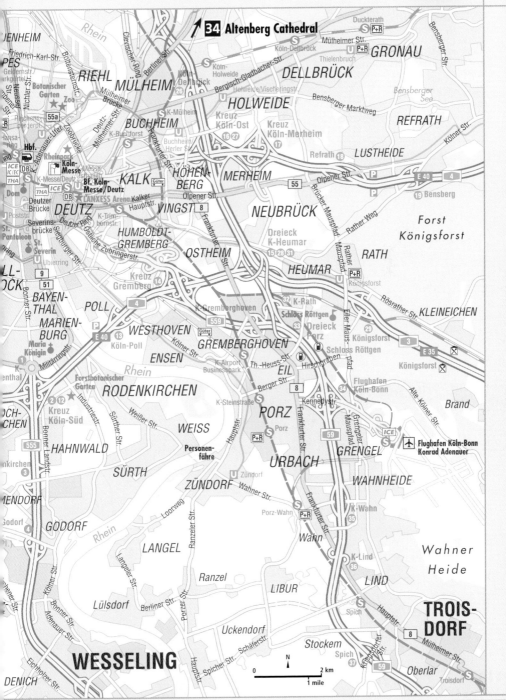

34 Altenberg Cathedral

Below from left: Altenberg Cathedral invites moments of pause and reflection. The church building, completed in the 14th century, is decorated in a relatively simple fashion, although the size of the west window would inspire feelings of insignificance in any visitor.

INFO Altenberg Cathedral

This former Cistercian abbey, called the "Bergisch" cathedral, is a Gothic building flooded with light.

Eugen-Heinen-Platz 2, Odenthal; Tel. (021 74) 45 33; 9.00–19.00, daily (except Friday mornings); S-Bahn to Bergisch Gladbach, then take bus connection.

Although its name might lead you to suspect otherwise, the Bergisch cathedral was never a bishop's seat. In the 12th century the counts of Berg donated their former ancestral seat in Altenberg to the Cistercian monastic order, who then began construction of the monastery of Altenberg in nearby Dhünn valley. The simple lines of the Gothic abbey, built between 1259 and 1379, are reminders of the modesty of the Cistercian order: there is no spire, merely a simple ridge turret on the roof. Simple Gothic lancet windows allow sunlight to flood into the plain interior. One notable feature is above the west portal: the largest church window in Germany, it is 18 m (60 feet) high by 8 m (27 feet) wide. Dissolved and secularized in the 19th century, since 1857 the church has been a "Simultankirche", serving both Protestants and Catholics as a place of worship. Concerts are also held here.

THE HIGHLIGHTS: AROUND COLOGNE

INFO Schloss Augustusburg

Countless windows on the garden side of the house permit views of abundant greenery, fit for a prince; Cologne's spiritual and temporal rulers have created a worthy summer residence (below). The interior is characterized by delicate rococo features (right).

Late baroque opulence located south of Cologne – a must for any lover of beauty!

Schlossstr. 6, Brühl; Tel. (022 32) 440 00; Tues–Fri 9.00–12.00, 13.00–16.00, Sat, Sun, public holidays 10.00–17.00; closed Dec/Jan, except for guided tours; U-Bahn or train to Brühl-Mitte.

In 1984, Schloss Augustusburg country house, the principal tourist attraction in the little town of Brühl, between Cologne and Bonn, was inscribed by UNESCO in its list of World Heritage Sites, and it is easy to see why. This magnificent building is considered a German masterpiece of rococo architecture. Intended as a summer residence for Cologne's prince elector, Clemens August, construction work was begun in 1725 and completed four decades later. Architects and artists from Germany, France, and Italy created a harmonious setting to showcase the staircase designed by Balthasar Neumann. Above imposing marble and stucco, the magnificent fresco "The Magnanimity and Generosity of Clemens August" adorns the ceiling. The Augustusburg park and grounds are typical for the time and are laid out on strict geometric lines.

Schloss Falkenlust's interior (below from left) reveals the ornate decorative style popular when it was built; the princes loved the art of hunting, typified by this wall painting with a falconry scene. The spirit of the baroque lives on in the dining room and bedrooms: a view of the upper salon (far right).

Just like Schloss Augustusburg, the smaller hunting lodge of Schloss Falkenlust is also a UNESCO World Heritage Site. The two rococo buildings lie only 1.5 km (a mile) apart and it is an easy stroll between them. Falkenlust was built between 1729 and 1737 and neither its name nor location are coincidental; herons would fly past here on their way to the Rhine, and Clemens August delighted in hunting them with falcons from the gardens of the house. After hunting, the Prince Elector, who was also the Archbishop of Cologne, would relax with his guests in the house, some of whose rooms are decorated with Chinese lacquerwork. Visitors who were not taking part in the hunt had a good view of events from a platform and could also survey the imposing park and its fountains. Among the illustrious guests at Falkenlust were such personalities as Mozart and Casanova.

THE HIGHLIGHTS:
AROUND COLOGNE

INFO Brauweiler Abbey

A view between the columns in the Brauweiler Abbey cloister (below); the abbey's main tower, flanked by two smaller towers (inset below), is a peculiarity. The spacious baroque inner courtyard is large enough for a good stroll (right).

A Romanesque pillar basilica with three aisles, west of Cologne; visit here to complete your Romanesque education begun in the city!

Ehrenfriedstr. 19, Pulheim; Tel. (022 34) 9 85 42 40; 10.00–18.00, daily; U-Bahn to Junkersdorf, bus connection from there.

In the Middle Ages it was common practice for the nobility to endow their own monasteries. Mathilde, the daughter of Emperor Otto II, and her husband, Count Palatine Ezzo, erected an abbey on their estate at Brauweiler to the west of Cologne, and donated it to the Benedictine order in 1024.

The 69-m (227-foot) high spires, the octagonal quatrefoil tower, and the two flanking side towers of the Romanesque St Nicholas's abbey church are visible from afar. Several pillars in the interior of the church betray traces of medieval paintwork. Among Brauweiler Abbey's notable features are the medieval cloisters and several baroque buildings.

After secularization at the beginning of the 19th century, the abbey buildings were used variously as a poorhouse, as a Gestapo prison during the Nazi period, and later as a psychiatric clinic.

A size comparison between excavator and human shows just how much "brown gold" is mined every day (below). The excavators in the Garzweiler I mine, north-west of Cologne, are among the largest mobile machines in the world (below inset). After the diggers have done their work only devastated landscape remains, taking decades to return to its natural state. The Garzweiler I mine alone has exposed 66 sq. km (26 square miles) of ground (right).

LIGNITE MINING IN VILLE

Today this area is one of lakes and woods for the people of Cologne to relax in, but until the middle of the 1960s it was filled with pits and slag heaps. Lignite was mined in the Ville hills for nearly a hundred years: the coal seams lay near the surface and needed only to be dug up. In the open-cast mine of Hambach, further to the north, giant excavators had to dig through several hundred metres (more than 700 feet) of sand, gravel, and loess sediment to reach the precious fuel. Germany's largest open-cast mine has been worked since 1978 and around 250 million cubic m (8.1 billion cubic feet) of material are removed every year, yielding 40 million tons of coal. It is intended that the mine will eventually cover 85 sq. km (33 square miles); so far less than half of this has been excavated. Several villages have had to be settled elsewhere to permit further digging work. From the adjacent Sophienhöhe hill, the visitor's gaze is drawn down into a crater that over the years has grown to a depth of 350 m (1,150 feet). Sophienhöhe hill itself, rising 200 m (660 feet) above the surrounding landscape, consists entirely of slag from the mine and is a popular destination for excursions. Those wishing to find out more about lignite mining on the Rhine should follow the "Strasse der Energie" ("energy road"), whose various sections provide a wide range of information about electricity generation from lignite.

COMPACT
COLOGNE

Cologne, once the "Rome of the north", is amongst the most popular destinations for city breaks in Germany – and the locals love their town as well. There are festivals to be celebrated and strolls to be taken, in the Old Town and on the banks of the Rhine, and bars in which to enjoy Kölsch and Rhineland cooking. Cologne's theatres and museums have a varied program, and the music and cabaret scene has something for every taste. Summer is unimaginable without "Kölner Lichter", the big illuminations and firework festival, and there is always the "fifth season": *Karneval*, or the Cologne Carnival.

Christopher Street Day is celebrated in a relaxed manner.

Comedy in the old "Harald Schmidt Show" studios.

Museums, music, and drama

Hänneschen Theater
One of the most traditional of Cologne's puppet theaters. Hänneschen and a cast of Cologne characters have many an adventure – all in Cologne dialect!
Eisenmarkt 2–4;
Tel 258 12 01.
www.haenneschen.de

Museum für Angewandte Kunst
The Museum of Applied Art houses one of Germany's most comprehensive collections of applied art from the Middle Ages to the present.
An der Rechtschule; Tel 22 12 67 35; 11.00–17.00, Tues–Sun. www.museenkoeln.de/ museum-fuer-angewandte-kunst

Musical Dome
Sell-out musical productions, as well as concerts and guest performances of all kinds, delight fans from all over Germany in an eye-catching modern building of blue glass and steel that can't be missed.
Goldgasse 1;
Tel (02 11) 577 90.
www.musical-dome.de

Philharmonie
The home of the Gürzenich orchestra and the nationally famous WDR Symphony Orchestra hosts concerts by many renowned artists every year. The concert program is varied and includes great works of symphonic and chamber music as well as jazz, folk, and pop.
Bischofsgartenstr. 1;
Tel 28 02 80.
www.koelnmusik.de

Festivals and events

Christopher Street Day/ Cologne Pride
The climax of this three-day lesbian and gay street festival is the CSD parade through the middle of the city. Since 2002 Cologne Pride has organized a wider program in the weeks preceding the parade with sports tournaments, a festival of culture, discussion groups, and a party.
Beethovenstr. 1;
Tel 169 09 88; end Jun–beginning Jul.
www.csd-cologne.de

c/o pop
When Popkomm left Cologne and the Ringfest was cancelled, c/o pop became the new festival for electronic music, indie, pop, and club culture in 2004. About a dozen venues feature 200 artists over five nights.
Tel 95 43 91 90;
Aug.
www.c-o-pop.de

Expedition Colonia
For three weeks during this festival about the city, guides offer tours with unusual topics, visiting places that are new even to born-and-bred locals.
Tel 65 09 77 77;
Apr.
www.expedition-colonia.de

Köln Comedy Festival
German and international comedians perform on various stages over 17 days in Germany's largest comedy event. The climax is the German Comedy Prize ceremony. Categories include Best Comedy Improv and Best Film Comedy.
Tel 65 09 65 01; Oct/Nov.
www.koeln-comedy.de

Kölner Lichter/Cologne Lights
Four tons of fireworks are fired into the night skies over Cologne as a convoy of 50 illuminated boats sails from Porz to Mülheim, applauded by delighted and astounded crowds.
Tel (021 71) 38 01;
Jul.
www.koelner-lichter.de

Kölner Sommerfestival/ Cologne Summer Festival
The Philharmonic has bridged the gap left by its summer break with a summer festival of internationally famous events including dance and musical theater.
Bischofsgartenstr. 1; summer holidays;
Tel 20 40 80.
www. koelnersommerfestival.de

Kölner Theaternacht
An evening where 30 venues offer theater fans samples of drama, cabaret, and dance. A bus shuttle service provides comfortable transport between them.
Oct.
www.theaternacht.de

Kölner Weinwoche/ Cologne Wine Week
Vintners from various German wine-growing areas present their wares over ten days to a thirsty Cologne audience.
Neumarkt/Heumarkt;
Tel 130 07 66;
May.
www.koelner-weinwoche. de.

lit.COLOGNE
Literature takes over Cologne for ten days. More than 130 readings by authors, debates, and dramatized readings are

OLD TOWN (CENTER)

You'll find further expert tips here to complement the sights described in the "Highlights" section (pp. 24–77). Please note that the area code for Cologne is **02 21**.

held in well-known and sometimes unexpected venues.
Tel 160 18 19;
end Feb/beginning Mar.
www.litcologne.de

Lange Nacht der Kölner Museen (Cologne's late night openings)
A "long night" in which about 40 of Cologne's cultural establishments stay open into the small hours to welcome an audience interested in art. The exhibitions are augmented with music, literature, film, dance, and drama; in 2007 there were 20,000 people in attendance. Five guided tours offered.
Maastrichter Str. 49;
Tel 95 15 41 19; Nov.
www.museumsnacht-koeln.de

MusikTriennale Köln
Once every three years, Cologne is taken over by contemporary music. Renowned stars and hotly tipped

"4711" Eau de Cologne is a local classic.

newcomers play old favorites and new pieces at some 30 venues, with a comprehensive background program of exhibitions, lectures, debates, and films.
Tel 925 71 60; Apr/May.
www.musiktriennalekoeln.de

Sommerblut Festival
Founded only in 2003, the exhibitions, comedy, readings, cabaret, chanson, concerts, and drama in this international festival of culture have become a firm date in the city's cultural calendar.
May–Jul.
www.sommerblut.net

Sommer Köln/Summer in Cologne
Artists from around the world present concerts and spectaculars at a variety of venues in the summer holidays. The motto for the last 20 years has been "open air and free entry". Considerable range of events for children.
Tel 169 09 88; in the summer holidays.
www.sommerkoeln.de

Straßenkarneval/ Street Carnival
The Carnival's relaxed atmosphere means that special rules obtain in Cologne between Women's Carnival and Ash Wednesday. Famed throughout the country, the Street Carnival begins on Women's Carnival Day at 11.11 and the madness builds to its climax with the Rose Monday procession.
Tel 57 40 00.
www.koelnerkarneval.de

Christmas Markets
No less than eight markets tempt the visitor to Cologne

Dressing up at the Cologne Carnival; a guard of honor.

for a pre-Christmas stroll. The largest is on Neumarkt Square, the most unusual on a boat on the Rhine promenade.
26 Nov–23 Dec, 11.00–21.00, daily.
www.koeln.de/tourismus/weihnachten/weihnachtsmaerkte-index.html

Sport and leisure

Cologne-Düsseldorf Rhine Trips
Whether on an hour-long sightseeing trip or a cruise of several days, there is much to see along the Rhine. The Kölsch discos and Majorca parties are legendary.
Frankenwerft 35;
Tel 208 83 18. www.k-d.de

Ford Cologne Marathon
Thanks to its route through the heart of the city, the Cologne marathon is considered one of the most beautiful in Germany. A half marathon and marathons for rollerbladers, handbikers, and walkers take place on the same day.
Tel 33 77 73 11;
Octobe.,
www.koeln-marathon.de

DKV Bridge Run
The popular run covers a distance of exactly 15.2 km

(9.5 miles) and crosses five bridges in Cologne. Competitors start and finish at the Chocolate Museum.
Tel 719 91 60.
www.asv-koeln.de

Holmes Place Health Club
A fitness and health club with a range of services. Located in the middle of the Old Town.
Gürzenichstr. 6–16;
Tel 598 14 14;
Mon–Thurs 7.00–23.00, Fri 7.00–22.00, Sat, Sun, public hols 9.00–20.00.
www.holmesplace.de

Shopping

4711
An internationally famous Cologne classic for two centuries, the "4711 Echt Kölnisch Wasser" Eau de Cologne company, on its original premises in the Glockengasse, offers a great selection of perfumes, lotions, potions, soaps, and wipes – beautifully gift-wrapped, of course.
Glockengasse;
Tel 57 28 92 50;
Mon–Fri 9.00–19.00, Sat 9.00–18.00.
www.4711.com

Cologne Souvenirs
Original Cologne souvenirs, bric-a-brac, and mementos to

Sünner im Walfisch brewery bar.

In the brewery bars, the "Köbes" brings fresh Kölsch.

suit every taste and price range.
Alter Markt 55;
Tel 257 04 57;
Mon–Sat 10.00–20.00, Sun 11.00–20.00, Jan–Mar 11.00–22.00, Sun 11.00–19.00, Apr–Dec.
www.cologne-souvenirs.de

Deko-Festartikel Schmitt
Cologne is the home of Carnival. Whatever the season, you'll find costumes, masks, wigs, and everything you need for a celebration at Schmitt's.
Johannisstr. 67;
Tel 12 36 87; Mon–Fri 10.00–19.00, Sat 11.00–15.00.

Messing-Müller
Every variety of metal and brassware has been sold here for the last 230 years. Nowadays this specialist store for tableware and cutlery concentrates on

exclusive accessories for the lifestyle of discerning buyers.
Minoritenstr. 1;
Tel 208 13 26; Mon–Fri 10.00–19.00, Sat 10.00–18.00. www.dekoschmitt.de

Pauls GmbH
This store near the Cologne Opera House is famous throughout the city and sells dance and ballet materials. The range encompasses points and pumps in all sizes and fashionable dance accessories.
Streitzeuggasse 6;
Tel 257 37 97; Mon–Fri 19.00, Sat 10.00–16.00.
www.paulsballett.de

Eating and Drinking

Alt Köln am Dom
Good atmosphere, traditional menu, and drinks, a popular bar right next to the cathedral.
Trankgasse 7, Tel 13 74 71.

Max Päffgen Brewery
A popular traditional bar that is never empty. In good weather you can relax in comfort in the pleasant beer garden to the rear of the bar, or stand at the tables in front and observe the comings and goings on Heumarkt Square.
Heumarkt 62;
Tel 257 77 65;
Tue–Sun 11.00–0.30.
www.max-paeffgen.de

Bierhaus en d'r Salzgass
Even though cask beer has been poured here only since 2003 – after a gap of a hundred years – this bar has already established a place for itself in the heart of the Old Town. The bustle in the bar can be viewed from the gallery above.
Salzgasse 5–7;
Tel 800 19 00; from 12.00 daily.
www.bierhaus-salzgasse.de

Brauhaus Sion
Tradition is valued in this large brewery bar, and several saloons tempt visitors to stay for a cool beer.
Unter Taschenmacher 5–7;
Tel 257 85 40; 10.30–0.30 daily.
www.brauhaus-sion.de

Brauhaus Sünner im Walfisch
A small bar area and a restaurant spread over two floors, with many nooks and corners. Groups can choose between a "Pittermänn-chen" (10 l/18 pint keg) or mini kegs of 3 or 5 l (6–9 pints). Situated in a fine old step-gabled building.
Salzgasse 13;
Tel 257 78 79; Mon–Thurs from 17.00, Fri from 15.00, Sat, Sun from 11.00.
www.walfisch.net

El Chango
Argentinian steak house in the middle of the Old Town. Wagon wheels divide the rooms, and you can sit among these and enjoy huge Argentinian steaks and excellent South American wine.
Bolzengasse 9;
Tel 258 12 12;
Mon–Fri, Sun 12.00–14.00, 18.00–24.00, Sat 18.00–24.00.
www.elchango.com

Haxenhaus zum Rheingarten
A historic tavern on the Rhine promenade, offering its patrons local cuisine, the best home-made sausages, and, of course, every preparation of shanks and leg joints as well as tasty Kölsch.
Frankenwerft 19;
Tel 257 79 66;
Sun–Thur 11.30–1.00, Fri, Sat 11.30–3.00.
www.haxenhaus.de

Holtmann's Restaurant
You're spoilt for choice in this bar, with a wide selection of seafood. The restaurant is usually full, with customers from all over the world.
Am Bollwerk 21;
Tel 257 63 30;
12.00–24.00, daily.
www.holtmanns.com

Rosendorn
The excellent Spanish tapas and agreeable conversation would soon make you forget you were in Cologne – if it were not for the view of the Ostermann fountain, with its carved figures.
Ostermannplatz;
Tel 257 52 69;
Mon–Fri from 16.00, Sat, Sun from 12.00.
www.rosendorn-koeln.de

OLD TOWN (CENTER)

You'll find further expert tips here to complement the sights described in the "Highlights" section (pp. 24–77). Please note that the area code for Cologne is 02 21.

Weinhaus Brungs

If you don't drink beer, choose from around two dozen wines instead. The interior of this 12th-century merchant's house reveals a magnificent spiral staircase leading to splendid galleries; beneath these, a dimly lit cellar offers cozy dining. The little terrace is particularly attractive.
Marsplatz 3–5;
Tel 258 16 66;
12.00–24.00, daily.
www.weinhaus-brungs.de

Accommodation

Alter Römer

Most of the rooms in this simple hotel have a direct view of the Rhine. There is also an excellent in-house restaurant.
Am Bollwerk 23;
Tel 258 18 85.

Das kleine Stapelhäuschen

Not only can you eat well in this down-to-earth building

The Hotel Maritim lobby.

on the Rhine promenade, you can sleep well here too; the tower room is particularly attractive (and has its own crane!).
Fischmarkt 1–3;
Tel 257 78 62.
www.koeln-altstadt.de/
stapelhaeuschen

Domhotel

A traditional, elegant five-storey building in a prominent position near the cathedral, offering the highest level of comfort in an exquisite setting.
Domkloster 2a;
Tel 202 40.
www.domhotel.de

Hotel an der Philharmonie

A family-run hotel that has recently been refurbished. Guest rooms and suites are comfortable and are decorated in modern and Mediterranean styles.
Große Neugasse 36–38;
Tel 258 06 79.
www.hadpc.de

Hotel Römerhafen

A cozy hotel with a nice view of the Rhine. Situated in the heart of the city, its gables form part of the famous Old Town skyline.
Am Bollwerk 9–11;
Tel 258 06 84.
www.hotel-roemerhafen.de

Maritim Hotel

This seven-storey luxury hotel on the banks of the Rhine rises like a ship above the water. The glass-roofed entrance hall is 100 m (330 feet) long and its many boutiques, bars, and restaurants lend it a sophisticated, cosmopolitan air.
Heumarkt 20;
Tel 202 70.
www.maritim.de

The Weinhaus Brungs serves a good drop.

Nightlife

Biermuseum

This is the place for beer drinkers: 19 different cask beers and over 30 bottled beers tempt locals and visitors alike to drink and celebrate.
Buttermarkt 39;
Tel 257 78 02;
14.00–3.00, daily.

Em Streckstrump

There is live music every evening in Germany's oldest jazz bar. An LED display at the entrance records with a certain pride how many gigs have taken place at the Streckstrump: at the time of publication, over 13,750.
Buttermarkt 37;
Tel 257 79 31;
20.00–3.00; daily.
www.papajoes.de

Flanagan's

An Irish pub with a varied program awaits visitors in the basement of the Alter Markt: students party during the week, on Saturdays there's dancing for everyone, and karaoke takes place on Sundays.
Alter Markt 36;
Tel 257 06 74;
Mon–Thurs 19.00–1.00, Fri, Sat 19.00–3.00, Sun 15.00–1.00.

Hard Rock Café

One of three German Hard Rock Cafés, some people are so intimidated by the collection of famous musicians' guitars and gold discs that they forget to drink.
Gürzenichstr. 8;
Tel 272 68 80;
Sun–Thurs 12.00–1.00, Fri, Sat 12.00–2.00.
www.hardrock.com

Kunibert der Fiese

With its rather uninspired décor but a superb location (right on the Rhine promenade), this "Aloha" cocktail bar has a good selection of cocktails and mixers. They also have Kölsch, of course.
Am Bollwerk 1–5;
Tel 925 46 80;
Sun–Thurs 8.00–1.00, Fri, Sat 8.00–3.00.
www.kunibertderfiese.de

Wiener Steffie

A meeting place for locals and visitors who are really in the mood for rocking out to German music. The themed nights, such as the "Bachelor Auction" or the "Night of Sin", are legendary.
Quatermarkt 5,
Gürzenichpassage;
Tel 257 69 00;
Fri, Sat, and nights before public hols 20.00–5.00.
www.wiener-steffie.com

Museums, music, and drama

Käthe-Kollwitz-Museum
The most comprehensive collection of the artist's works includes sculpture, drawings, lithographs, and posters.
Neumarkt 18–24;
Tel 227 28 99;
10.00–18.00, Tues–Fri, 11.00–18.00, Sat, Sun.
www.kollwitz.de

Kölnischer Kunstverein/ Cologne Art Association
One of the oldest art societies in Germany, showing temporary exhibitions of international contemporary art.
Die Brücke, Hahnenstr. 6; Tel 221 21 70 21;
13.00–19.00, Tues–Fri, 12.00–18.00, Sat, Sun.
www.koelnischerkunstverein.de

Kölnisches Stadtmuseum/ City History Museum
An informative collection illustrating the history and everyday life of Cologne and its inhabitants since the Middle Ages: Cologne cliques, Kölsch, Carnival, and Kölnisch Wasser.
Zeughausstr. 1–3;
Tel 22 12 57 89;
10.00–17.00, Wed–Sun , 10.00–20.00, Tues.
www.museenkoeln.de/ koelnisches-stadtmuseum

Kolumba
The archdiocese's art museum, with 2,000 years of western culture. St Columba's new buildings, designed by Peter Zumthor, combine medieval and contemporary art and architecture.
Kolumbastr. 2–4;
Tel 257 76 72;
12.00–17.00, Wed–Mon.
www.kolumba.de

NS-Dokumentations- zentrum
An archive of documentation illustrating the Nazi period in Cologne, situated in the EL-DE-Haus, a former Gestapo prison.
Appellhofplatz 23–25;
Tel 22 12 63 32;
10.00–18.00, Tues–Fri, Sat, 11.00–16.00, Sun.
www.museenkoeln.de/ ns-dok

Opera House
The city opera house has a varied program, and the building is an interesting example of Adenauer-era 1950s architecture.
Offenbachplatz;
Tel 22 12 84 00.
www.buehnenkoeln.de

Schauspielhaus
The municipal theater, right behind the opera house, with a large repertoire of classic and modern plays.
Offenbachplatz;
Tel 22 12 84 00.
www.buehnenkoeln.de

Theater am Dom
This theater by the cathedral is one of the leading companies in Germany. Many popular stars and actors from the world of television and film appear here in contemporary and often boisterous comedies.
Glockengasse 11 (Opern Passagen);
Tel 258 01 53.
www.theateramdom.de

Festivals and events

Bierbörse/Beer Exchange
The "beer exchange" is a three-day opportunity to celebrate Germany's favorite drink. A great variety of beers from around the world can be sampled in rows of beer gardens, and music and entertainment provide a background to the boozy atmosphere.
Tel (021 71) 38 01; Aug.
www.bierboerse.com

Cologne Conference SPIEGEL Television & Film Festival
Germany's leading festival for non-mainstream television. Successful series like *Sex and the City* and *24* received their German premiere here.
Tel 454 32 80; Sept/Oct.
www.cologneconference.de

Herbst KunstFilmBiennale/ Autumn Art Film Festival
The autumn art film biennial, a cross between a festival and an exhibition unique to Cologne, shows feature-length and short films at the cutting edge of art and cinema.
Tel 226 57 45; Sept/Oct.
www.kunstfilmbiennale.de

Short Cuts Cologne
Some 180 shorts, ranging from short fiction through animation to experimental film and documentaries are shown over five days at this international short film festival presented by the Kölner Filmhaus.
Kölner Filmhaus,
Maybachstr. 111;
Tel 22 27 10 27; Nov/Dec.
www.short-cuts-cologne.de

Sport and leisure

The Cable Car
For decades children and adults have been entranced by the journey over the Rhine in the cable car (*Seilbahn*). The seven-minute journey covers 930 m (half a mile) and affords unusual views of Cologne and the Rhine.
Zoo Station: Riehler Str. 180;
Rheinpark Station,
Sachsenbergstr./corner of Auenweg; Tel 547 41 83;
April–first week of Nov 10.00–18.00, daily.
www.koelner-seilbahn.de

Beauty-Body-Wellness- Lounge
Beauty to the exclusion of all else in the Belgian Quarter: classic facial, eyebrow, and lashes treatments, manicure, pedicure.
Brüsseler Str. 55;
Tel 257 12 12;
Mon–Fri 11.00–20.00, Sat 11.00–16.00.
www.schoenseinschmitz.de

Lindner Hotel Dom Residence
A luxurious oasis of health and beauty above the roofs of Cologne. The wellness and fitness area with its indoor pool, whirlpool, Kneipp pool, sauna, and solarium is open to hotel guests and non-residents.
Stolkgasse/An den Dominikanern 4a;
Tel 164 40.
www.lindner.de

Samudra
Stress reduction and preventive health treatments in beautiful surroundings. Visitors can float in blood temperature salt-water isolation booths, unique in Cologne. A great selection of high quality massages.
Brabanter Str. 4;
Tel 250 99 49;
10.00–22.00, daily.
www.samudra.de.

Savoy Health Club
The wellness and beauty area of the Savoy Hotel offers

Inset from left: St Kunibert and the television tower; Romanesque windows adorn St Kunibert; St Gereon; the Hohenzollern Bridge; the impressive main hall of Cologne Hauptbahnhof.

OLD TOWN (NORTH)

You'll find further expert tips here to complement the sights described in the "Highlights" chapter (pp. 78–91). Please note that the area code for Cologne is **02 21**.

whirlpools, Roman steam baths, Finnish saunas, a rock grotto with massage jets, and an oriental rhassoul steam bath, as well as massages. Staying the night in one of the five spa suites with a private whirlpool is pure luxury.
Turiner Str. 9;
Tel 162 33 33;
10.00–23.00, daily.
www.savoy.de

Shopping

Apropos Cöln – The Concept Store
Designer fashion, jewellery, and accessories with fashionable labels, as well as cosmetics and lifestyle books are to be found in this unusual store in the exclusive Mittelstrasse. Appropriate relaxation after a day's shopping is to be found in the restaurant, bar, and day spa.
Mittelstr. 12;
Tel 272 51 90; Mon–Sat 10.00–20.00.
www.apropos-coeln.de.

Besteckhaus Glaub
Europe's only specialist cutlery store. Silver, gold, stainless steel, or horn-handled: there is something for every taste among their 500 designs in various patterns and styles. Their in-house workshop can restore or complete valuable heirloom pieces and canteens.
Komödienstr. 107;
Tel 13 41 36;
Tues–Fri 10.00–18.00, Sat 10.00–14.00.
www.besteckhaus-glaub. com

Bruno Wolkenaer
This famed specialist store has had an excellent reputation among amateur

and professional artists for nearly 100 years, and sells varnishes, paints, paper, and brushes, as well as easels and canvases.
Ehrenstr. 6; Tel 25 32 88;
Mon–Fri 10.00–19.00, Sat 10.00–18.00.
www.wolkenaer.de

Città di Bologna
If you wish to be just ahead of the herd and wear fashionable designer clothes, at the prices to match, this is the place for you.
Flandrische Str. 2;
Tel 925 58 16;
Mon–Fri 11.00–20.00, Sat 11.00–18.00.

Dunkles Gold Schokoladen
The "dark gold" chocolate store offers chocolate of the highest quality, including exceptionally fine brands such as Amedei, Domori, and Quai Sud, as well as drinking chocolate and chocolate cake decorations.
Brüssler Str. 44;
Tel 258 59 00;
Mon–Fri 11.00–19.00; Sat 11.00–16.00.
www.dunklesgold.de

Eiting Räume
A team of interior designers, decorators, and upholsterers will design a whole room for you, from new upholstery for the sofa to the carpets or an exquisite wall hanging. A great selection of high-quality materials.
Aachener Str. 7;
Tel 510 35 45;
Mon–Fri 10.00–19.00, Sat 10.00–16.00.

Filz Gnoss
Woollen cloth milled with soap and warm water produces felt, an ideal raw material for all sorts of

products. The store has an enormous selection, ranging from classic slippers through table sets and mats to decorating and DIY supplies.
Apostelnstr. 21;
Tel 257 01 08;
Mon–Fri 9.30–18.30, Sat 10.00–16.00.
www.filz-gnoss.de

Gliss Caffee Contor
You can smell the coffee as soon as you enter this store, which will sell you the best coffee varieties in the world.
St.-Apern-Str. 14–18;
Tel 250 83 83;
Mon–Fri 9.30–18.30, Sat 11.00–18.00.
www.gliss.de

Globetrotter
The Cologne branch of this outward-bound specialist offers an almost unique range of everything you could possibly need to survive in the great outdoors. The old Olivandenhof galleries have been converted into water sport pools, cold and rain chambers, and climbing tunnels for outdoors fans.
Olivandenhof, Richmodstr. 10; Tel 277 28 80;
Mon–Thurs 10.00–20.00, Fri, Sat 10.00–21.00.
www.globetrotter.de

Hack
Bags made from Swiss tents and army surplus blankets, but also high-quality tailored leather jackets and trousers are part of the selection in this odd store. You can be measured up by the in-house designers for leather trousers, should you so wish.
Maastrichter Str. 22;
Tel 240 92 21;
Mon–Fri 10.00–19.00, Sat 11.00–16.00.
www.lederware.de

Jürgen Eifler
In his workshop, Eifler creates high-quality bespoke classic hats and caps. His specialist store stocks all kinds of headgear, including a few odd sorts.
Friesenwall 102a;
Tel 25 45 35;
Mon–Fri 11.00–18.00, Sat 11.00–16.00.
www.hut-classic.com

Kölner Rum Kontor
Rum lovers can expect 300 varieties of high-octane cane sugar spirits here.
Lübecker Str.;
Tue–Fri 10.00–18.00, Sat 11.00–14.00.
www.koelnerrumkontor.de

Laden 13
A great range of choice jewellery at reasonable prices. The selection includes silver in modern designs, set stones, and pearls, plus a gold collection.
Gertrudenstr. 13;
Tel 257 81 61;
Mon–Fri 11.00–19.00, Sat 11.00–18.00.

Musikhaus Tonger
A treasure house for musicians, from instruments to sheet music, tabs, and accessories: everything to gladden a musician's heart.
Breite Str. 2–4;
Tel 925 47 50;
Mon–Fri 10.00–19.00, Sat 10.00–18.00.
www.musik-tonger.de.

Nachbar Beauty Hair Accessories
A professional wet shave is no problem in Cologne's only establishment specializing in male grooming. Anyone wishing to do it himself can purchase shaving brushes,

strops, and cut-throat and safety razors.
Breite Str. 161;
Tel 257 45 67;
Tues–Fri 9.00–18.00, Sat 9.00–16.00.

Parfümerie P. Möltgen
All the leading brands of cosmetics, care products, and fragrances for men and women are sold on the four floors of this specialist boutique. The prices are usually 20 percent below the standard retail price.
Ehrenstr. 55;
Tel 257 32 08;
Mon–Wed 10.00–19.00, Thurs, Fri 10.00–20.00, Sat 10.00–18.00.
www.parfuemerie-moeltgen.de

Schirm Bursch
Umbrellas and parasols abound in this store. Many of the umbrellas and walking sticks are made bespoke in the in-house workshop.
Breite Str. 104;
Tel 257 80 57;
Mon–Fri 10.00–18.30, Sat 10.00–15.00.

Susanne Ritzenhoff
Designer clothes at very reasonable prices; Susanne Ritzenhoff specializes in second-hand designer fashion.
Pfeilstr. 24;
Tel 258 19 49;
Mon–Fri 11.00–18.00, Sat 11.00–16.00.

Worms
This boutique has been Cologne's number one for exclusive lingerie and elegant swimwear for nearly 75 years. The exceptionally competent staff will advise you in a very agreeable setting.
Neumarkt 33; Tel 21 39 19;
Mon–Fri 10.00–19.00, Sat

10.00–16.00 (Nov/Dec until 18.00).
www.dessous.com

Eating and drinking

Alfredo
One of the best Italian restaurants in the heart of the city. Enjoy live music on Fridays, when the head chef, a trained singer, performs arias from Italian operas.
Tunisstr. 3; Tel 257 73 80;
Mon–Fri 12.00–15.00 and 18.00–23.30, Sat 12.00–15.00.
www.ristorante-alfredo.com

Chez Chef
A smart open-plan restaurant with a well-dressed clientele drawn from the surrounding offices during the week and the cinemas on the ring road's amusement strip at the weekend. The cuisine is based on Mediterranean and new German dishes.
Spichernstr. 77;
Tel 650 36 50;
Mon–Fri 11.00–1.00, Sat from 18.00.
www.chez-chef.de

Heising und Adelmann
A culinary destination for lovers of fresh fish dishes, combined with a smart and busy bar.
Friesenstr. 58–60;
Tel 130 94 24;
Mon–Sat from 18.00.
www.heising-und-adelmann.de

La Strada
A cozy place to knock back coffee during the day and freshly poured Kölsch in the evenings, fortifying yourself for the demands of a fun-filled evening ahead on the town.

Hohenzollernring 13;
Tel 25 18 65;
Mon–Thurs, Sun 10.00–4.00, Fri, Sat 10.00–5.00.
www.lastrada-koeln.de

L'Escalier
An excellent small restaurant concentrating on modern and light cuisine. Ostentatious décor has been deliberately avoided and the chef's watchword is "regional and seasonal".
Brüsseler Str. 11;
Tel 205 39 98;
Tues–Fri 12.00–14.00 and 18.30–22.00, Mon, Sat 18.30–22.00.
www.lescalier-restaurant.de

Le Moissonnier
A relaxed and excellent restaurant, where fine dining does not require dressing up; a glance at the menu reveals exclusive creations by a French head chef. The bistro-style décor quickly makes you forget you are in Cologne and not in Paris.
Krefelder Str. 25;
Tel 72 94 79;
Tues–Sat 12.00–15.00 and 19.00–24.00.
www.lemoissonnier.de

Limbourg
A small and refined restaurant in the so-called "Bermuda Triangle" of the Belgian quarter. The brick walls lend a Mediterranean air that corresponds entirely to the French-Mediterranean cuisine. The menu changes weekly. A table here is prized, so it is best to book well in advance. Try the fennel baked in ginger and potato gratin.
Limburger Str. 35;
Tel 250 88 80;
Tues–Sun 19.00–0.30.
www.limbourg.mynetcologne.de

Max Stark
A small cozy bar with a raised ground floor. The beer is fresh from the tap, served by nice waiting staff in a good atmosphere.
Unter Kahlenhausen 47;
Tel 200 56 33; from 11.00, daily. www.max-stark.de

Stüsser
A pleasant local bar (known well beyond the immediate area) dispensing fresh Kölsch and home-made tonic wine, as well as hearty bar snacks; the menu changes daily.
Neusser Str. 4; Tel 72 72 53;
10.00–1.00, daily.
www.stuessersbrauhaus.de

Waschsalon
You can happily sit and drink coffee beneath washing machine drums in this odd bar, or even have a snack. This all-rounder cafe is full of young people wishing to see and be seen.
Ehrenstr. 77; Tel 13 33 78;
Sun–Thurs 10.00–1.00, Fri, Sat 10.00–3.00.

Accommodation

Antik Hotel Bristol
Centrally located near the MediaPark, this privately run hotel has large rooms with furnishings from the 18th and 19th centuries.
Kaiser-Wilhelm-Ring 48;
Tel 12 01 95.
www.antik-hotel-bristol.de

Central Hotel am Dom
The rooms of this recently refurbished three star hotel are of an international standard. There are exclusive restaurants and lots of shopping nearby.
An den Dominikanern 3;
Tel 13 50 88.
www.centralamdom.de

Inset from left: The cathedral and the Hohenzollern Bridge; the interior of St Gereon; the façade of the Hotel Excelsior Ernst, illuminated by night; the light show at Fifi Choo attracts night owls.

You'll find further expert tips here to complement the sights described in the "Highlights" chapter (pp. 78–91). Please note that the area code for Cologne is **02 21**.

Excelsior Hotel Ernst
One of the best hotels in the city; guests have been waking up to a view of the cathedral here for the last 140 years. The luxurious hotel has rich trappings and valuable antiques, and provides pure indulgence in the shadow of the cathedral's spires.
Trankgasse 1–5; Tel 27 01.
www.excelsiorhotelernst.de

Good Sleep
Those on a limited budget will find simple but good accommodation here, near the cathedral and the main station.
Komödienstr. 19–21;
Tel 257 22 57.
www.goodsleep.de

Hostel Station
A low-budget hotel for backpackers near the station. Rooms range from singles to six-bed dorms.
Marzellenstr. 44–48;
Tel 912 53 01.
www.hostel-cologne.de

Hotel Cristall
Just a stone's throw from St Ursula's, the design is unexpectedly eccentric; each room has a differing individual design concept.
Ursulaplatz 9–11;
Tel 163 00.
www.hotelcristall.de

Hotel Viktoria
This elegant hotel is housed in one of Cologne's most beautiful classical listed buildings. Its tasteful and noble interior is decorated with marble walls, columns, and alcoves as well as skilfully executed stucco work.
Worringer Str. 23;
Tel 973 17 20.
www.hotelviktoria.com

Nightlife

Diamonds
An elegant club with a smart international clientele. Relax in one of four different bars when you're not on the dance floor.
Hohenzollernring 90;
Tel 160 86 20; Fri, Sat, and evenings before public hols 22.00–5.00.
www.club-diamonds.de

Dollhouse
A party atmosphere: stag parties and business types in particular enjoy the American table-dancing. On Fridays, so-called "Ladies' Night", men get the chance to dance for a change.
Hohenzollernring 92;
Tel 139 33 83; Fri, Sat 21.00–5.00.
www.dollhouse-cologne.de

Downtown Club
If you don't have time for their "Afterwork-Party" on Thursday, go on Friday for the "Funky-Party" or Saturday for the "Hip-Hop-Party".
Brabanter Str. 15;
Tel 510 47 83; Thurs 17.00–1.00, Fri, Sat 22.00–5.00.
www.downtownclub.de

EdelPink
A young crowd, sitting in pink-decorated cellar rooms, listening to house music, and being served drinks by scantily clad waiting staff.
Brabanter Str. 9;
Tel 01 78 / 5 54 47 73;
Tue–Thurs 21.00–3.00, Fri, Sat 21.00–5.00.

Fifi Choo
R&B and illuminated disco balls for a young crowd. Wear the wrong clothes and you won't get past the bouncers.
Hohenzollernring 89–93;
Tel 56 98 10; Tues 20.00–4.00, Fri, Sat 22.00–5.00.
www.fifichoo.de.

Goldfinger
Smart Bond girls meet cute secret agents and celebrate their cosmopolitan lives.
Friesenstr. 54;
Tel 130 77 73;
Mon–Thurs 20.00–3.00, Fri, Sat 20.00–5.00.
www.goldfinger-koeln.de

Klapsmühle
Party till you're carried out: this club is infamous for the many singles parties held here.
Hohenzollernring 39–41;
Tel 257 12 27;
Mon, Wed from 21.00, Fri, Sat 21.00–5.00.
www.klapsmuehle.com

Lauschgift
A scene for mainly younger people, who drink and dance the night away to house, electro, RnB, hip-hop, and Latin music.
Aachener Str. 50;
Tel 550 00 60.
www.lauschgift-koeln.de.

Lotte Haifischbar
It won't just be sailors who are spoilt for choice by the range of cocktails.
Im Klapperhof 41; Tel 13 13 35; 20.00–5.00, daily.
www.lotte-haifischbar.com

Petit Prince
One of the oldest and most famous European dance clubs. Couples dance here to Latin American music on Mondays, Wednesdays, and Saturdays, while on Thursdays predominantly black music is played. Dance lessons quickly teach you the necessary steps before the themed nights.
Hohenzollernring 90;
Tel 12 25 20.
www.petitprince.de

Roxy
If after a long night of partying you've still not had enough drinking and celebrating, or if you're still on your own, this is the right place.
Aachener Str. 2; Tel 25 19 69; Sun–Wed 24.00–5.00, Thurs–Sat 24.00–6.00.

Spirits
Delicious cocktails and long drinks are mixed here in a totally relaxed atmosphere. A rotating team of DJs play delightful and obscure music at moderate volumes; even the non-alcoholic drinks are divine and highly recommended.
Engelbertstr. 63;
Tel 473 36 25;
Tues–Thurs 20.30–2.00, Fri, Sat 21.00–3.00.
www.spiritsbar.net

triple a club
Well-off, smart twenty-somethings lounge about to a garish light show and freshly dispensed house music.
An d'r Hahnepooz 8;
Tel 277 56 80 80;
Tues, Thurs from 22.00, Wed from 21.00, Fri, Sat from 23.00.
www.triplea-club.de

Vic
A cocktail bar with decidedly elegant décor, reminiscent of a classic hotel bar. Vic attracts a mostly young, social crowd who enjoy the stylish surroundings. A good pre-clubbing venue.
Friesenstr. 16; Tel 13 51 16;
Tues–Thurs 19.00–2.00, Fri, Sat 19.00–3.00.
www.vic-bar.de

Museums, music, and drama

Comedia
This small and unconventional theater offers cabaret, music, and acting lessons for amateurs. The Ömmes & Oimel children's theater is always popular with its younger visitors.
Löwengasse 7–9;
Tel 399 60 10.
www.comedia-koeln.de

Galerie Michael Werner
One of Germany's most respected galleries, with exhibitions by artists such as Jörg Immendorff and A.R. Penck. Its thematic focus is German contemporary art but it also exhibits modern masterpieces in general.
Gertrudenstr. 24–28;
Tel 925 46 20.
www.michaelwerner.de

Museum Schnütgen
One of the world's most important collections of medieval art is displayed in the dignified setting of St Cecilia's Church.
Cäcilienstr. 29;
Tel 22 12 36 20;
10.00–17.00, Tues–Fri,
11.00–17.00 Sat, Sun.
www.museenkoeln.de/museum-schnuetgen

Rautenstrauch-Joest Museum
One of Germany's most important ethnological museums, exhibiting the art and culture of non-European people. The collection comprises 65,000 objects and 100,000 photographs.
Josef-Haubrich-Hof;
Tel 33 69 40.
www.museenkoeln.de/rautenstrauch-joest-museum

Festivals and events

Dä längste Desch vun Kölle
"The longest bar in Cologne": one of Germany's largest street parties, not noticeably lacking in Kölsch or local cuisine.
Serviusstrasse, Severin-Kirchplatz, Chlodwigplatz;
third weekend Sep.

Romanische Nacht
An extended "Romanesque night" of old music held in the basilica of St Maria im Kapitol. Every two years the "Romanesque Summer" sees other churches converted into concert halls.
St Maria im Kapitol,
Kasinostrasse entrance,
Richartzstr. 2–4;
Tel 22 12 38 05; end July.
www.romanischer-sommer.de

Sport and leisure

Agrippabad
Whereas most of the recreational swimming pools are outside the heart of the city, this pool is near the Neumarkt. There is a wave pool, a four-seasons pool, and a giant slide, as well as a range of saunas, a gym area, and lots of open-air space.
Kämmergasse 1;
Tel 279 17 30;
Bathing: Mon–Fri 6.30–22.30, Sat, Sun, public hols 9.00–21.00; Sauna: Mon–Fri 9.00–23.00, Sat, Sun 9.00–21.00.
www.koelnbaeder.de

Mauritius-Therme
This health spa complex in the heart of the city is part of a hoTel Hotel residents and visitors to the saunas and thermal pools will find relaxation and peace in the middle of the city.
Mauritiuskirchplatz 3–11.
www.mauritius-ht.de

Shopping

Engelelf
This mall stocks everyday and designer products by young European designers and brands. An extensive range includes one-offs and small runs of fashionable bags, cushions, and tablecloths, as well as accessories.
Engelbertstr. 11;
Tel 492 91 48; Tues–Fri 14.00–19.00, Sat 11.00–17.00. www.engelelf.de

Honig Müngersdorff
A well-established family business specializing in honey and honey-related products, including honey-flavoured spirits and mead, as well as beeswax candles and natural cosmetics.
An St Agatha 37; Tel 925 90 50; Mon–Fri 9.00–18.00, Sat 9.30–14.00.
www.honig-muengersdorff.de

Jotjelunge
Costumes and disguises for Carnival and other social events and festivities.
Lindenstr. 53;
Tel 24 98 91; Mon–Fri 12.00–19.00, Sat 10.00–14.00.
www.jotjelunge.de

Krupka
A shoe store stocking fashionable and exclusive creations of exceptional quality.
Merowinger Str. 26;
Tel 304 98 60; Mon–Fri 10.00–19.00, Sat 10.00–16.00.
www.krupka-schuhe.de

Tanger
This store exudes an exotic waft of the Orient. An immense selection of choice spices, baked goods, Arab delicacies, tea flavours, and exotic unguents complement the range.
Pantaleonswall 30;
Tel 278 96 18;
Mon–Thurs 9.00–13.00, 14.00–19.00, Fri 10.00–12.00, 15.00–19.00, Sat 10.00–16.00.
www.tanger-markt.de

Tausend Fliegende Fische
A store selling trendy clothes and fashion by young labels and brands; in the student quarter, mostly frequented by young people.
Roonstr. 16; Tel 240 02 33;
Mon–Fri 10.00–20.00, Sat 11.00–18.00.

Eating and Drinking

Brauhaus Pütz
A cozy old brew bar near Rudolf Square. Freshly poured Kölsch, just like in the Old Town, and hearty bar snacks on the menu.
Engelbertstr. 67; Tel 21 11 66; from 16.30, daily.

Capricorn i Aries
An excellent small restaurant in the south of the city. A path of rose petals leads the way to culinary delights to the palate. There are only four tables so reservations are essential.
Altenburger Str. 34; Tel 32 31 82; Tues–Sun from 19.00.
www.capricorniaries.com

Früh em Veedel
A subsidiary of the brewery by the cathedral. For people from the south of the city, Veedels-Früh is almost an institution. After dining on

Inset from left: Everything you need to know about chocolate and advertising of every kind in the Chocolate Museum; the German Sports and Olympic Museum; Rheinauhafen dockside; the west side of St Pantaleon.

OLD TOWN (SOUTH)

You'll find further expert tips here to complement the sights described in the "Highlights" chapter (pp. 92–107). Please note that the area code for Cologne is 02 21.

typical Cologne cuisine, a home-made schnapps is recommended for the digestion.
Chlodwigplatz 28; Tel 31 44 70; Mon–Sat 11.00–1.00. www.frueh. de

Haus Töller
The tables here have been polished with a scrubbing brush and soft soap for a hundred years. A cozy place serving Hämchen (cooked pork knuckle) and Rhineland braised beef.
Weyerstr. 96; Tel 258 93 16; Mon–Sat from 17.00. www.haus-toeller.de

Kap am Südkai
The view from the giant glass façade of this bar is an incomparable panorama of the newly refurbished Rheinauhafen dock area.
Agrippinawerft 28; Tel 35 68 33 33; Mon–Fri 10.00–24.00, Sat, Sun 12.00–24.00. www.kapamsuedkai.de

Kurfürstenhof
South city residents occasionally drop into this bar-restaurant near Chlodwigplatz Square for Italian-inspired cuisine.
Bonner Str. 21; Tel 331 92 16; 9.00–2.00, daily.

La Société
A gourmet restaurant in the middle of the student quarter serving culinary surprises; for example, soups are served from the "soup chemist's" in test tubes. A Cologne institution since the 19th century.
Kyffhäuser Str. 53; Tel 23 24 64; 18.30–23.00, daily. www.lasociete.info

La Vision
An exclusive restaurant on the 11th storey of the 130-year-old water tower. Top chefs prepare creations that have earned the restaurant a Michelin star.
Kaygasse 2; Tel 200 80; Tues–Sat 12.00–14.00 and 19.00–22.00. www.hotel-im-wasserturm. de

Spielplatz
A popular and well-known bar. There are regular theater and music performances in the back room.
Ubierring 58; Tel 31 47 50; Mon–Fri 11.00–2.00, Sat 17.00–2.00, Sun 17.00–1.00. www.spielplatz-lokal.de

Accommodation

Ambassador Hotel
The Ambassador is among Cologne's best-regarded hotels. Its central location suits it to business travellers and holidaymakers.
Barbarossaplatz 4a; Tel 921 52 00. www.ambassador.de

Crown Plaza Cologne City Center
A ten-storey hotel on Rudolfsplatz Square with more than 300 rooms.
Habsburgerring 9–13; Tel 22 80. www.crowneplaza.de

Hopper Hotel et cetera
A hotel hidden behind the massive walls of a pre-existing 19th-century monastery. The monks' former cells are now considerably more luxurious than they once were.
Brüsseler Str. 26; Tel 92 44 00. www.hopper.de

Hotel Ahl Meerkatzen vun 1264
A hotel offering every modern comfort and relaxation in one of the city's oldest buildings. From here, a meerkat could reach the cathedral and main station in a single bound.
Mathiasstr. 21; Tel 397 57 90. www.meerkatzen-koeln.de

Hotel im Wasserturm
The celebrated French interior architect Andrée Putman has created one of Germany's most unusual hotels here. Situated within the walls of the listed water tower, the hotel offers the ultimate in luxury. Even Brad Pitt was impressed when he visited.
Kaygasse 2; Tel 200 80. www.hotel-im-wasserturm.de

Nightlife

Blue Shell
A legendary meeting place for the indie and punk scene. DJs play cool music if no gigs are on.
Luxemburger Str. 32; Tel 23 20 34; Sun–Thurs 20.00–2.00, Fri, Sat 19.00–4.30. www.blue-shell.de

Haifischclub
With over 100 drinks on offer, patrons really are spoilt for choice.
Im Ferkulum 24–26; Tel 310 33 06; Mon–Thurs 20.00–2.00, Fri, Sat 20.00–4.00. www.haifischclub.de

Pacific Bar
One of the few really good bars in the student quarter. Both the ingredients and the mixing are right.
Kyffhäuserstr. 17; Tel 923 11 60; Mon–Thurs 20.00–1.00, Fri, Sat from 20.00. www.pacificbar.de

Roonburg
A vaulted cellar in the studenty Bermuda Triangle. Highlights here include a cheesy song night, Kölsch night, and "Börsencrash", stock market crash night, when the drinks prices are determined by demand.
Roonstr. 33, Tel 240 37 19; Tues from 21.00, Thurs–Sat from 22.00. www.roonburg.de.

Rose Club
A cool club with British music situated somewhere between northern soul and pop. A meeting place for twenty-somethings.
Luxemburger Str. 37; Tel 240 82 66; Tues–Thurs 22.00–5.00, Fri, Sat 23.00–5.00. www.rose-club-cologne.de

Shepheard
Smart customers match the décor and drink both classic cocktails and the house's creations. To reach cocktail heaven, visit the cellar.
Rathenauplatz 5; Tel 331 09 94; Tues–Sat 20.00–3.00. www.shepheard.de

Tsunami Club
Here they'll play anything from punk to thrash metal, as long as it's loud.
Im Ferkulum 9; Tel 801 63 34; gigs from 20.00, parties Wed–Sat from 21.00 or 22.00. www.tsunami-club.de

Museums, music, and drama

ARTheater
A theater company that shows its own productions and features guest performances. The scary midnight horror readings are legendary.
Ehrenfeldgürtel 127; Tel 550 33 44.
www.artheater.info

Galerie Christian Nagel
Whether painting, photography, video art, or installations: all the art here has a socio-political stance.
Richard-Wagner-Str. 28; Tel 257 05 91; 11.00–18.00, Mon–Sat.
www.galerie-nagel.de

Kölner Karnevalsmuseum
Cologne's Carnival Museum is without doubt the largest in the German-speaking world.
Maarweg 134–136; Tel 574 00 76; 10.00–20.00, Thurs, 10.00–17.00, Fri, 11.00–17.00, Sat, Sun.
www.kk-museum.de

Literaturhaus Köln
Cologne's literary institute holds readings by famous and less well-known authors, features lectures on all aspects of reading and writing, and supports young writers.
Schönhauser Str. 8; Tel 995 55 80.
www.literaturhaus-koeln.de

Museum für Ostasiatische Kunst
Cologne's Museum of East Asian Art has art and crafts from China, Japan, and Korea. Opened in 1913 as the first specialist museum of its kind, since 1977 it has been housed in a classic modernist building.

Universitätsstr. 100; Tel 22 12 86 08; 11.00–17.00, Tues–Sun, 11.00–20.00, Thurs.
www.museenkoeln.de/muse um-fuer-ostasiatische-kunst

Studiobühne Köln
The studio stage of the oldest university theater company in Germany alternates home productions with international guest appearances.
Universitätsstr. 16a; Tel 470 45 13.
www.studiobuehne-koeln.de

Theater im Bauturm
Contemporary plays and well-known and popular classics alternate in the schedule here. Their adaptation of Patrick Süskind's *Double Bass* has delighted audiences for 25 years.
Aachener Str. 24–26; Tel 951 44 31.
www.theater-im-bauturm.de

Volkstheater Millowitsch
Despite Willy Millowitsch's death, this traditional folk theater continues to bring the Cologne sense of the ridiculous to the stage. Peter Millowitsch is the seventh generation to lead the family company.
Aachener Str. 5; Tel 25 17 47. www.millowitsch.de

Festivals and events

Mittelalterlich Phantasie Spectaculum
For one summer weekend the area around the Fühlinger See lake is transformed by this lively event which transports visitors back to the 13th century.
Fühlinger See;
Tel (025 08) 16 03; Aug.
www.spectaculum.de

Summerjam
One of the biggest European reggae festivals. International and local stars have been appearing over three days at the Fühlinger See lake for the last 23 years.
Fühlinger See;
Tel (07 11) 238 50; three days beginning Jul.
www.summerjam.de

Sport and leisure

Aqualand
Aqualand on the Fühlinger See lake has something for everyone: a range of saunas, thermal baths, a mineral pool, and a sea salt grotto to relax in, a fitness studio, indoor and outdoor pools for movement therapy, and a play area for the children.
Merianstr. 1; Tel 702 80; Mon–Thurs 9.30–23.00, Fri 9.30–24.00, Sat 9.00–24.00, Sun 9.00–23.00.
www.aqualand.de

Finkens Garten
Five hectares (12 acres) of Rodenkirchen devoted to 123 bird species and countless insects.
Friedrich-Ebert-Str. 49; Tel 285 73 64; Sat, Sun, public hols 6.00–18.00.
www.stadt-koeln.de

Forstbotanischer Garten/ Botanic Gardens
A meadow of peonies, a valley of rhododendrons, a heath garden, and a Japanese garden are just some of the highlights of a journey of discovery through this arboretum.
Schillingsrotter Str. 100; Tel 35 43 25; Apr to Aug 9.00–20.00, Jan, Feb, Nov, Dec 9.00–16.00, Mar, Sep, Oct 9.00–18.00.
www.stadt-koeln.de

Galopprennbahn/ Racecourse
The Weidenpesch racecourse offers a chance to experience exciting gallop races close up. The Happy Family race day in July is especially popular with parents and children.
Rennbahnstr. 152; Tel 974 50 50.
www.koeln-galopp.de

Kletterfabrik/ Climbing Walls
A 1,000 sq. m (11,000 square feet) of climbing walls in the suburb of Ehrenfeld.
Lichtstr. 25; Tel 502 99 91; Mon–Fri 10.00–23.00, Sat, Sun 10.00–21.30.
www.kletterfabrik-koeln.de

Naturfreibad Fühlinger See
Cologne's biggest lake is an Eldorado for sun worshipers, divers, anglers, surfers, rowers, and canoeists.
Stallagsbergweg; Tel 279 18 50; Mon–Fri 10.00–18.00, Sat, Sun 9.00–18.00.
www.koelnbaeder.de

Neptunbad
A visit to this refurbished art nouveau pool is a must for all health and architecture enthusiasts. Ehrenfeld's first public bath house was used as a public pool until the 1990s before being re-opened as a "Health Club & Spa" in 2002. No club membership is required to use the sauna area.
Neptunplatz 1; Tel 71 00 71; 9.00–24.00, daily.
www.neptunbad.de

Öffentliche Kölner Golfsportanlage/ Public Golf Course
The other side of the elite golf clubs, Cologne's public golf course in Roggendorf-

GREENBELT, THE LEFT BANK OF THE RHINE

You'll find further expert tips here to complement the sights described in the "Highlights" section (pp. 108–127). Please note that the area code for Cologne is **02 21**.

Thenhoven is open to beginner and expert alike.
Parallelweg 1; Tel 78 40 18; Mon 12.00–21.00, Tues–Fri 8.00–21.00, Sat, Sun, public hols 7.30–21.00.
www.koelner-golfsportanlage.de

ran Fitnessclub
The complex has three saunas indoors and one outdoors, an outdoor pool, five plunge pools, and 2,000 sq. m (22,000 square feet) of gardens.
Kronstädter Str.; Tel (022 34) 70 09 90; Mon–Fri 8.00–23.00, Sat, Sun 8.00–22.00.
www.ran-fitnessclub.de

Stadionbad/Outdoor Pool
Stadionbad has eight indoor and outdoor pools for your diving and swimming pleasure.
Aachener Str./Stadion; Tel 279 18 40; in summer Mon–Fri 10.00–20.00, Sat, Sun, public hols 9.00–20.00.
www.koelnbaeder.de

Shopping

Balloni
Balloni stocks a giant selection of balloons in every style and shade, and you'll find unlimited ideas for household decorations, parties, and festivities of every kind.
Ehrenfeldgürtel 88–94; Tel 51 09 10; Mon–Fri 9.30–19.00, Sat 9.30–16.00.
www.balloni.de

Magazin
If you want a certain amount of functionality in your interior décor, you're in the right place here; almost everything from lamps to chairs is plain, solid, and hardworking.
Aachener Str. 40–44; Tel 82 03 00; Tues–Fri 10.00–19.00, Sat 10.00–16.00.
www.magazin-koeln.de

Eating and Drinking

Assisi
Lovers of Italian cuisine are drawn to one of the best restaurants in the deep south of the city.
Sürther Hauptstr. 157; Tel (022 36) 693 85; Tues–Sun 18.00–22.00.
www.ristorante-assisi.de

Bellini
A daily specials board joins the standard menu in inviting you on a culinary journey through the cuisine of la bella Italia.
Bonner Str. 328; Tel 38 70 68; from 12.00 and from 18.30, daily.
www.bellini-ristorante.de

Bootshaus Alte Liebe
You can watch onshore pedestrians and river-borne boats from this houseboat moored on the towpath at Rodenkirchen.
Rodenkirchener Leinpfad 10; Tel 39 23 61; 11.00–24.00, daily.
www. bootshaus-alteliebe.de

Braustelle
Cologne's smallest and most inventive brewery has a beer menu that changes monthly, as well as their home-made "Helios" wheat beer and "Ehrenfelder Alt" dark beer.
Christinastr. 2; Tel 285 69 32; 18.00–1.00, daily.
www.braustelle.com

Em golde Kappes
Brewery in the northern suburb of Nippes; a rendezvous for locals and a pleasant venue for visitors.
Neusser Str. 295; Tel 73 49 32; Mon–Sat 10.00–24.00.

Früh im Haus Tutt
Freshly poured cask beer and other hearty drinks with down-to-earth music, right in the middle of Ehrenfeld.
Fridolinstr. 72; Tel 502 82 80; 17.00–24.00, daily.
www.haus-tutt.de

Haus Scholzen
This solid old restaurant has been serving Cologne and seasonal dishes as part of the culinary scene in Ehrenfeld for a century. The speciality is the Ehrenfeld mustard roast.
Venloer Str. 236, Tel 51 59 19; Wed to Sat 11.30–15.00 and 17.00–24.00.
www.haus-scholzen.de

Haus Unkelbach
A brewery tap bar with decent bar food. Fried soured kidneys, fritters, and sauerkraut soup are a tasty basis for a boozy night. During the summer there are 200 tempting seats in the beer garden.
Luxemburger Str. 260; Tel 41 41 84; Mon–Fri 17.00–24.00, Sat, Sun 11.00–1.00.
www.hausunkelbach.de

Landhaus Kuckuck
Exquisite dining among cuckoo clocks and fine furniture in the room Müngersdorf keeps for best.
Olympiaweg 2; Tel 48 53 60; Tues–Sat 12.00–23.00, Sun 12.00–18.00.
www.landhaus-kuckuck.de

Accommodation

Best Western Premier Hotel Regent
Four-star hotel in the western suburb of Braunsfeld. Nicely decorated with spacious rooms.
Melatengürtel 15; Tel 549 90. www.hotelregent.de

Brennerscher Hof
This country house-style hotel is an oasis of peace located in the western suburb of Junkersdorf. About half the rooms are suites and there is a boarding house apartment for guests wishing to stay for an extended period.
Wilhelm-von-Capitaine-Str. 15–17; Tel 948 60 00.
www.brennerscher-hof.de

Rheinkasseler Hof
Located in the north of the city, this four-star hotel promises relaxation from noise and bustle. Some of the rooms are in the 18th-century part of the building.
Amandusstr. 6–10; Tel 70 92 70.
www.rheinkasseler-hof.com

Nightlife

Die Kantine
A northern beacon for the dance-mad. Parties, gigs, specials, and outdoor events are all part of the service.
Neusser Landstr. 2; Tel 167 91 60; Tues from 20.00, Fri, Sat from 22.00.
www.kantine.com

Live Music Hall
If no criminally expensive concert by some international star is being held, this place is mainly filled with young night owls. Performances by some of the less well-known stars and singer-songwriters are also recommended. A large warehouse-style venue that can hold up to 1,500 people. When there is no live music event on, the DJs make the most of the powerful sound system.
Lichtstr. 30; Tel 954 29 90; Wed 20.00–2.00, Fri 21.00–4.00, Sat 22.00–4.00.
www.livemusichall.de

Museums, music, and drama

Kulturbunker Mülheim
The cultural spectrum in this former bunker ranges from punk gigs to exhibitions and film showings.
Berliner Str. 20; Tel 61 69 26. www.kulturbunker-muelheim.de

Festivals and events

Frühlingsvolksfest Deutz/ Cologne Spring Fair
Cologne's biggest spring fair will tempt you to take a daring trip on the "Wild Mouse" or a ride on the Ferris wheel.
*Festplatz Deutz, Siegburger Str. 66; Tel 51 98 83; after Easter.
www.gkseg.de*

Funkhaus Europa Summerstage/Summer World Music Festival
A world music festival with a different theme every year. The heart of the event is the open-air concert on the Saturday at the Tanzbrunnen fountain.
*Tanzbrunnen, Rheinparkweg 1, Stadtgarten, Venloer Str. 40; Tel 52 78 10; Jun/Jul.
www.summerstage.de*

SOMA
Nomen est omen – its name tells you everything: the Summer of Music and Art festival specializes in just that. A three-day festival in the Rheinpark featuring techno and indie, reggae, and world music: something for every taste.
*Jugendpark, in the Rheinpark under the Zoo bridge; Jul.
www.soma-festival.de*

Corpus Christi in Mülheimer
A traditional Corpus Christi procession on the Rhine. A festively decorated boat is joined by a flotilla of smaller and larger escorts on a trip down the river and greeted with an honor salute by a shooting club.
*Pastoralbüro St Clemens und Liebfrauen, Adamsstr. 15; Tel 96 70 20; Corpus Christi.
www.muelheimer-gottestracht.de*

Sport and leisure

Abenteuerhalle Kalk/Skate & Adventure Park
Kalk adventure hall and skate park is a rendezvous for BMX riders and rollerbladers. Those preferring something less speedy can attempt the climbing wall or work off their excess energy playing basketball.
*Christian-Sunner-Str.; Tel 880 84 08; Mon–Sat 15.00–22.00, Sun 15.00–20.00.
www.abenteuer-halle.de*

ANANDA
Germany's largest institute for tantra and massage, whose holistic massage techniques tempt visitors to a sensual journey around the body.
*Frankfurter Str. 40; Tel 608 65 85; 10.00–21.00, daily.
www.tantramassage.de*

Claudiustherme
Cologne's Rheinpark is home to one of the most beautiful thermal baths in Europe, fed by its own hot mineral spring. The enormous sauna area has everything from a Finnish sauna to herbal steam baths, and hot mud baths. The panorama sauna has a fantastic view of the park and Cologne Cathedral.
*Sachsenbergstr. 1; Tel 98 14 40; 9.00–24.00, daily.
www.claudius-therme.de*

Gut Leidenhausen
On Sundays you can see birds of prey up close on this estate in Porz-Eil that once belonged to a medieval knight. The rest of the time the bird sanctuary takes in sick and injured animals. Other interesting diversions include a forestry, a fruit museum, and a wildlife park.
*Porz-Eil; Tel (0 22 03) 399 87; Apr–Sept: Sun, public hols 10.00–18.00, Oct–Mar: Sun, public hols 10.00–17.00.
www.cologneweb.com/ greifvogelstation*

Naturfreibad Vingst
An old quarry has been turned into an attractive lake surrounded by meadows and planted beds. After swimming and diving, barbecues, football, and beach volleyball are the order of the day.
*Vingst, Vingster Ring; Tel 279 18 60; only in summer; Mon–Thurs 10.00–19.00, Fri–Sun, public hols 9.00–19.00.
www.koelnbaeder.de*

Rheinpark
This spacious park, first laid out for the National Flower Show in 1957, has retained its 1950s garden architecture. In 2007 it was even honored as Germany's most beautiful park. Look out for parrots, escapees from Cologne Zoo.
Rheinpark; right bank of the Rhine; south of the Zoo Bridge.

Eating and Drinking

Brauhaus Goldener Pflug
A typical Cologne brewery and a meeting place for friends and neighbors in what used to be a luxury restaurant. The Kölsch and the food taste particularly good in the giant beer garden from April to September.
*Olpener Str. 421; Tel 310 56 31; Mon–Sat 16.00–24.00, Sun 11.30–24.00.
www.brauhaus-goldener-pflug.de*

Brauhaus ohne Namen
A brewery without a name, but with an unexpectedly Old Town feel in the middle of Deutz. The old central ballroom has blossomed into a very popular place to meet.
*Mathildenstr. 42; Tel 81 26 80; Mon–Fri 16.00–24.00, Sat, Sun 11.30–24.00.
brauhaus-ohne-namen.de*

Deutzer Bahnhof
This restaurant situated in Deutz's historic old railway station is a draw for locals and trade fair delegates alike. The balcony-like little galleries are particularly charming, as are the spacious terraces outside, illuminated with strings of lights.
*Ottoplatz 7; Tel 880 06 15; Mon–Thurs 11.00–1.00, Fri, Sat 11.00–3.00, Sun 10.00–1.00.
www.deutzerbahnhof.de*

Graugans
Gourmet restaurant in the Hyatt Regency Hotel specializing in fine Euro-Asian cuisine, with a 40-page wine list taking you on a journey through the world's best wine regions. The view of the Old Town lying opposite is

THE RIGHT BANK OF THE RHINE

You'll find further expert tips here to complement the sights described in the "Highlights" section (pp. 128–143). Please note that the area code for Cologne is **02 21**.

incomparable. Reservations essential.
Kennedy-Ufer 2a;
Tel 82 81 17 71;
Tues–Sat 18.30–22.00.
www.cologne.regency.hyatt.
de

HoteLux
Soviet bar decorated with Soviet relics. The shade of red predominates apart from the inevitable vodka and Soviet cocktails; the menu offers a changing selection of dishes from the former Soviet bloc.
Von-Sandt-Platz 10;
Tel 24 11 36;
Sun–Thurs 18.00–1.00, Fri, Sat 18.00–3.00.
www.hotelux.de

Mongo's
The Mongo's chain has eight restaurants, all dedicated to Mongolian cuisine, and this one is in the basement of the KölnTriangle tower block. A stroll to aid digestion is recommended and best taken on the roof terrace, which has a view of the cathedral on the opposite bank of the Rhine.
Ottoplatz 1;
Tel 989 38 10;
Mon–Thurs 12.00–24.00, Fri, Sat 12.00–1.00, Sun 12.00–16.00, 17.00–24.00.
www.mongos.de

Rheinterrassen
After standing empty for decades this building was re-occupied in 1999. From inside you can observe the wonderful view of the Rhine through large peepholes, and outside in the charming beer garden you are nice and close to the river.
Rheinparkweg 1;
Tel 65 00 43 21;
Tues–Sat 18.00–1.00, Sun 12.00–17.00 and 18.00–1.00.
www.rhein-terrassen.de

Restaurant Isenburg
Where once robber barons held court, gourmets now dine. The Isenburg's tree-lined approach road and the moat around its historic walls make just arriving here an experience. Fine French cuisine rules the classical dining room, accompanied by a selection of French wines.
Johann-Bensberg-Str. 49;
Tel 69 59 09;
Tues–Fri 12.00–15.00 and 18.30–24.00, Sat 18.00–24.00.
www.isenburg.info

Zur Tant
The finest Austrian cuisine has been served in this half-timbered house in Langel, at the southern end of Cologne, for 30 years. Only the view of the Rhine is a reminder that you are not further south in the mountains.
Rheinbergstr. 49;
Tel (022 03) 818 83;
Fri–Wed 12.00–14.30 and 18.00–22.00.
www.zurtant.de

Accommodation

Holiday Inn am Flughafen
The airport Holiday Inn is a four-star business hotel with the usual high level of comfort you would expect from this global hotel chain.
Waldstr. 255;
Tel (022 03) 56 10.
www.koeln-bonn-airport-holiday-inn.de

Hotel Silencium
Located in the right-bank suburb of Brück, this privately run four-star hotel is an ideal resting place after a tiring trade fair – or a day of sightseeing. The hotel also has a spacious garden

terrace and a beautiful winter garden.
Olpener Str. 1031;
Tel 89 90 40.
www.silencium.de

Hotel Spiegel
A privately run hotel near the airport with all the comforts of a three-star establishment. If that's not enough, the nearby "Porzer Stadtwald" is a nature reserve and bird sanctuary where you can jog or stroll.
Hermann-Löns-Str. 122;
Tel (022 03) 96 64 40.
www.hotel-spiegel.de

Hyatt-Regency Köln
A first-class establishment in the best location on the right bank of the Rhine, with elegant and luxurious décor. The magnificent view of the Old Town should entrance even the local and international pop and rock stars, and other celebrities who stay here.
Kennedy-Ufer 2a;
Tel 828 12 34.
www.cologne.regency.hyatt.de

Insel Hotel
Charming family-run hotel in Deutz. The hotel is renowned for its large breakfast buffet and the nice hotel bar is rarely deserted. The hotel also offers a free shuttle service to the Claudius Therme health spa.
Constantinstr. 96;
Tel 880 34 50.
www.inselhotel-koeln.de

Kosmos Hotel
An individual and family-run four-star hotel in the right-bank suburb of Buchforst, popular with business travellers and cultural tourists. Not located in the best

area of the city, the short train ride into the center takes 10 minutes (3 stops), but the rooms are spacious with some English cable TV stations and are reasonable value.
Waldecker Str. 11–15;
Tel 670 90.
www.kosmos-hotel-koeln.de

Radisson SAS Hotel
Only a few minutes' walk from the Cologne trade fair, this futuristic-looking new complex combines bold design with modern elegance and décor. If you can afford it, the best place to stay is the Capitolium Suite, with 90 sq. m (970 square feet) of floor space.
Messekreisel 3;
Tel 27 72 00.
www.cologne.radissonsas.com

Nightlife

Bootshaus
More floor space than any other disco in Cologne, and situated directly under the Zoo Bridge. Dance in two large rooms or on the sand especially strewn outside the entrance. Top German and international DJs spin the discs and drive the audience wild.
Auenweg 173;
Tel 922 60 88;
Fri, Sat 22.00–7.00.
www.bootshaus.tv

Elektroküche
A techno and house music club in the right-bank docks area. Columns, low seating, and a real party on Fridays and Saturdays. Resident DJs are joined by guest DJs.
Siegburger Str. 110;
Tel (01 73) 938 93 28; Fri, Sat from 22.30.
www.elektrokueche.com

Musums, music, and drama

Bergisches Freilicht-museum Lindlar

An interesting open-air museum exhibiting historical forms of commerce, and Bergisch rural and artisanal work from the 19th and 20th centuries.
Lindlar, Schloss Heiligenhoven; Mar–Oct 10.00–18.00, Tues–Sun, Nov–Dec 10.00–16.00, Tues–Sun, Jan, Feb only for special exhibitions.
www.bergisches-freilichtmuseum.lvr.de

Max-Ernst-Museum Brühl

The museum houses an exhibition of paintings, drawings, and sculptures by the exceptional dadaist and surrealist artist Max Ernst, born in Brühl in 1891. There is a permanent exhibition and constantly changing loans from public and private collections.
Brühl, Comesstr. 42/Max-Ernst-Allee 1; Tel (018 05) 74 34 65; 11.00–18.00, Tues–Sun, first Thurs in month 11.00–21.00.
www.maxernstmuseum.lvr. de

Rheinisches Freilicht-museum Kommern

The Rhine open-air museum comprises 65 accurately reconstructed and original buildings demonstrating the architecture, lifestyle, and commerce of the rural population of the Rhineland since the 15th century.
Mechernich-Kommern, Auf dem Kahlenbusch; Tel (024 43) 998 00; Apr–Oct 9.00–18.00, daily, Nov–Mar 10.00–16.00, daily.
www.kommern.lvr.de

Rheinisches Industriemuseum

Rhine Industrial Museum is a conglomerate of historic factories, with workshops and machinery on six sites throughout the Rhineland illustrating the history of manufacturing over the last few centuries.
Oberhausen, Ratingen, Solingen, Bergisch Gladbach, Engelskirchen, Euskirchen; Tel (for all sites) (018 05) 74 34 65;
www.rim.lvr.de

Schloss Augustusburg

A rococo masterpiece, famed for Balthasar Neumann's staircase, and the favorite residence of Clemens August von Wittelsbach, Prince Elector and Archbishop of Cologne. The house, the baroque gardens, and the Falkenlust hunting lodge are all UNESCO world heritage sites (see p. 150).
Brühl, Schlossstr. 6; Tel (022 32) 440 00; 9.00–12.00, 13.30–16.00, Tues–Fri, 10.00–17.00, Sat, Sun.
www.schloss-bruehl.de

Festivals and events

Brühler Schlosskonzerte

Concerts take place through-out the summer against the historic backdrops of Schloss Augustburg, the Max Ernst Museum, and the Christus-kirche in Brühl.
Brühl, Schlossstr. 6; Bookings: Brühl, Bahnhofstr. 16; Tel (022 32) 94 18 84; May–Aug.
www.schlosskonzerte.de

Rheinkultur/Rhine Culture Festival

With the motto "outdoors and free", the one-day Rhine Culture festival has been attracting hordes of music fans since 1983.
Rheinaue Bonn, Gluckstr. 2; Tel (02 28) 207 08 06; Jul.
www.rheinkultur.com

Chivalry at Burg Satzvey

Every year in spring, gallant knights are called to tourn-aments here in one of the best-preserved moated cas-tles in the Rhineland. Sur-rounding the lists is a med-ieval market.
Burg Satzvey, Mechernich-Satzvey, An der Burg 3; Tel (022 56) 958 30; spring and Sept/Oct. www.burgsatzvey.de

Sport and leisure

Bronx Rock

Germany's largest climbing hall is situated at the gates of the city, welcoming climbers of all abilities.
Wesseling, Vorgebirgsstr. 5; Tel (022 36) 89 05 70; Mon–Fri 9.00–24.00, Sat, Sun, public hols 9.00–22.00.
www.bronxrock.de

Bubenheimer Spieleland

Many an adult has got lost in the maize maze; there is an adventure playground for fine weather and an all-weather hall for rainy days.
Nörvenich, Burg Bubenheim; Tel (024 21) 711 94; Mid–Mar–first week Nov 9.00–19.00, daily.
www.bubenheimer-spieleland.de

CaLevornia

A recreational swimming complex of 20,000 sq. m (215,000 square feet) with swimming pools and saunas.
Leverkusen, Bismarckstr. 182; Tel (02 14) 83 07 10; Mon–Fri 8.00–22.00, Sat, Sun 9.00–22.00.
www.calevornia.de

"De Bütt" Family Pool

This complex has a massage pool with a current channel and a 25 m (80 foot) sports pool; outdoors there are whirlpools and a salt-water pool, and a range of saunas.
Hürth, Sudetenstr. 91; Tel (022 33) 729 40; Swimming: Mon–Fri 6.30–21.00, Sat, Sun 9.00–21.00, Sauna: Mon–Fri 10.00–23.00, Sat, Sun 9.00–23.00.
www. familienbad-huerth.de

Freizeitzentrum Siebengebirge

Take some time off from the mundane in the Siebengebirge leisure complex saunas. The open-air swimming pool even has its own beach.
Königswinter-Oberpleis, Dollendorfer Str. 106–110; Tel (022 44) 921 70; Mon–Thurs 11.00–23.00, Fri 11.00–24.00, Sat 10.00–24.00, Sun 10.00–22.00. www. saunapark-siebengebirge. de

Fresh Open

A great massage and recreational pool complex with lots of outside space. The little ones will be delighted with the 101-m (333-foot) long water slide.
Frechen, Burgstr. 65; Tel (022 34) 95 64 15; Mon 10.15–21.30, Tues, Wed, Fri 6.30–21.30, Thurs 6.30–14.00, Sat 10.00–18.30, Sun 9.30–18.30.
www.fresh-open.de

Karlsbad Brühl

A recreational pool and leisure venue in Brühl with its own sauna complex and a range of health, beauty, and grooming services.
Brühl, Kurfürstenstr. 40; Tel (022 32) 70 22 70; Mon–Fri 10.00–22.00, Sun 9.00–20.00.
www. karlsbad-bruehl.de

AROUND COLOGNE

You'll find further expert tips here to complement the sites described in the "Highlights" chapter (pp. 144–157). Please note that the area code for Cologne is **02 21**.

Mediterana

A health and beauty village. A short stay in south Cologne will bring city folk rest and relaxation.
Bergisch Gladbach, Saaler Mühle 1; Tel (022 04) 20 20; 9.00–24.00, daily.
www.mediterana.de

Parksauna Bergheim

An oasis of pampering with ten different sauna environments. Swimming pools, whirlpools, saltwater jacuzzis, and underwater massage chairs are all available here in this beauty and fitness complex.
Bergheim, Johann-Ruland-Weg 1–3; Tel (022 71) 46 66; Mon–Fri 10.00–23.00, Sat, Sun, public hols 10.00–20.00.
www.parksauna.de

Michael Schumacher Kart- und Event-Center

If you want to chase round bends after the seven-time Formula One champion, you're in the right place here.
Kerpen-Sindorf, Michael-Schumacher-Str. 5; Tel (022 73) 601 90; Mon–Fri 12.00–23.00, Sat 10.00–23.00, Sun, public hols 10.00–22.30.
www.ms-kartcenter.de

Otto-Maigler-See

The lake has about 500 m (900 feet) of sandy beach where you can swim, sunbathe, knock back drinks, and, of course, people watch.
Hürth-Gleuel; Tel (022 33) 352 48; Mon–Fri 9.00–22.00, Sat, Sun, public hols 8.00–22.00.
www.otto-maigler-see.de

Panorama Park Sauerland

A nice wildlife and adventure park with 40 attractions welcoming you on an exciting journey of discovery.
Kirchhundem-Oberhundem, Rinsecker Str. 100; Tel (027 23) 77 41 00; open only in summer.

Phantasialand Brühl

The "Black Mamba", "Talocan", and "Winja's Fears" white-knuckle rides will raise the adrenalin levels of any passenger, but the little ones may prefer a gentle animal ride or a trip on the log flume. The extensive schedule of entertainments is rounded off with excellent shows by musicians and other artists.
Brühl, Berggeiststr. 31–41; Tel (022 32) 362 00; Mid–Mar–first week of Nov 9.00–18.00, daily, "Winter Dreams" on certain dates 11.00–20.00.
www.phantasialand.de

Sea Life Königswinter

A journey through aquariums tracing the Rhine from its source to where it joins the North Sea. One of the highlights is an underwater tunnel through the tropical section, allowing you to stroll beneath mighty rays and sharks.
Königswinter, Rheinallee 8/ Berliner Platz; Tel (022 23) 297 12; 10.00–18.00, daily.
www.sealifeeurope.com

Sommerrodelbahn Kommern

A sort of 680-m (1,250-foot) long giant slide in the Eifel region, open in the summer, which can be taken gently or at breakneck speed, depending on your preference.
Mechernich-Kommern, Zur Sommerrodelbahn; Tel (024 43) 98 13 80; Apr–Oct, 10.00–22.00, daily, Nov–Mar 10.00–18.00 Sat, Sun.
www.rodelbahn-kommern.de

Saunahof Hahn

Located in an 18th-century manor house, this establishment promises pure relaxation, with plenty of saunas, jacuzzis, pools, and even a nudist area.
Kerpen-Sindorf, Europaring; Tel (022 73) 989 70; Mon–Sat, holidays, 9.00–23.00, Sun 9.00–20.00
www.sauna-hof-hahn.de

Eating and drinking

Gut Lärchenhof

A first-class golf course to the west of Cologne, with a restaurant whose head chef's creations have earned it a Michelin star.
Pulheim-Stommeln, Hahnenstr.; Tel (022 38) 92 31 00; 12.00–14.00 and 18.00–22.00, daily.
www. restaurant-gutlaerchenhof. de

Restaurant Dieter Müller

Schloss Lerbach is home to a luxury hotel and an excellent gourmet restaurant. Chef Dieter Müller has three stars and serves only the best luxury food.
Bergisch Gladbach, Schloss Lerbach, Lerbacher Weg; Tel (022 02) 20 40; Tue–Sat 12.00–14.00 and 19.00–22.00.
www.schlosshotel-lerbach.com.

Vendôme im Grandhotel Schloss Bensberg

A restaurant boasting three Michelin stars. Extraordinary creations are conjured up in noble surroundings with a baroque atmosphere. The restaurant belongs to the hotel of the Schloss Bensberg. Situated on a hill, it is the perfect place to stay if you want to indulge yourself, or celebrate.
Bergisch Gladbach, Bensberg, Kadettenstr.; Tel (022 04) 42 19 41; Wed–Sun 12.00–14.00 and 19.00–22.00.
www.schlossbensberg.com

Accommodation

Hotel Schloss Friedestrom

This hotel situated in medieval Zons complements its historical setting with high-quality furnishings and Mediterranean accessories.
Dormagen-Zons, Parkstr. 2; Tel (021 33) 50 30.
www.friedestrom.de

Grandhotel Schloss Bensberg

Bergisch Gladbach's five-star hotel at the east gate of Cologne. Luxurious rooms, a three-star gourmet restaurant and a health spa.
Bergisch-Gladbach, Kadettenstr.; Tel (022 04) 420.
www.schlossbensberg.com

Nightlife

Tanztempel Amun & Gaudi

Shiny happy people dance beneath the gaze of the Pharaoh Tutankhamun.
Bergisch Gladbach, Johann-Wilhelm-Lindlar-Str. 25; Tel (022 02) 520 62; Fri, Sat, public hols from 22.00.
www. tanztempel-amun.de

Treppchen 2

Why go into town when you can take things to excess in the suburbs? Even Cologne city folk party here.
Pulheim, Siemensstr. 4, Tel (022 38) 63 93; Fri, Sat 22.00–5.00.
www.treppchen2.de

MAJOR MUSEUMS

From Roman treasures to the most up-to-date contemporary works, no German town has a cultural legacy of a breadth and depth to compare with that of Cologne. This metropolis on the Rhine is, after all, Germany's second-oldest city and every era has left its historic mark here. Although it has given its name to both an archdiocese and an electorate, Cologne has neither an archbishop's palace nor a prince elector's residence; it was the citizens who collected the art, and, later, it was the citizens who donated it back to their home town. Many of the museums in Cologne are thus not only temples to culture but also an expression of an exemplary sense of traditional civic pride.

A lot of glass inside and out: the museum planners wanted transparency, recording and emphasizing the connections between modern Cologne and its Roman past. This past is still visible in many places, for example the Hafenstrasse, which goes right past the museum.

INFO
*Römisch-Germanisches Museum,
Roncalliplatz 4,
Tel. (0221) 22 12 44 38,
Tues–Sun 10.00–17.00 ,
U-/S-Bahn to
Dom/Hauptbahnhof.*

The Dionysus Mosaic

The Dionysus Mosaic covers 70 sq. m (750 square feet) and consists of 1.5 million tiles of clay, glass, and natural stone. It once graced the dining room floor of a Roman villa probably belonging to a rich merchant. This world-famous mosaic is situated today in exactly the same place where it was laid in 220 BC.

The mosaic was named for the central depiction of Dionysus, the son of the father of all the gods, Zeus. Known as Bacchus in Roman Cologne, Dionysus was the god of

Drunk in the city centre: Dionysus/Bacchus.

wine and is portrayed here in this role, in a wine-induced haze and supported by an attendant.

The central picture is surrounded by octagonal images of concupiscent satyrs and the god of love, Amor, riding on a lion. It is among the most popular of all the exhibits in this museum and is a must-see for any visitor.

A chance find

As an air-raid shelter was being dug out near the cathedral in 1941, the excavations uncovered a sensation – to be precise, the walls of a Roman villa from the 3rd century and with them the Dionysus Mosaic (see sidebar). Following the exact footprint of the Roman villa, the architects Klaus Renner and Heinz Röcke designed a museum in 1974 whose form was as modern for its time as it was controversial. Next to the museum is preserved a section of the original Roman road to the docks. To complement the mosaic, the museum has

antiquities collections of the Wallraf-Richartz Museum and the Prehistoric Museum. The museum is much more than just a display case; it is both a venue for archaeological research and an archaeological archive for Cologne, displaying the underground legacy of the city and its hinterland from prehistoric times to the early Middle Ages.

Like the mosaic, one of the museum's other best-known works of art, the reconstructed monument to Lucius Poblicius (c. 40 BC), who served in the fifth legion, is visible through the enormous glass façade of the ground floor. Supported by columns, a small temple

sarcophagus. This tomb was also discovered by chance during excavation work, as were many other exhibits illustrating Roman day-to-day life.

It is not only the collection that has made the museum one of the most popular in Germany but also the presentation of the artefacts: the pieces are arranged thematically as well as chronologically, affording an insight into everyday Roman life that history buffs will seldom find elsewhere.

Delicate glasswork

Pieces of Roman buildings, portraits, ceramics, and

The Römisch-Germanisches Museum in Cologne houses the largest collection of Roman glassware in the world, with an amazing variety of form and function.

acquired some three million other finds that originally formed part of the

building in which individual figures are distinguishable stands on the actual

frescoes are arranged with architectural models to illustrate how a small colony

RÖMISCH-GERMANISCHES MUSEUM

Experience Cologne's Roman past first hand, in both great works of art and in everyday objects; the museum's emphasis is on the documentation of quotidian Roman life. The museum has outdoor annexes including parts of the Roman city walls and the Roman tower on St Apernstrasse, the cemetery underneath St Severin's Church in the south of the city, and the Roman sepulchre in the suburb of Weiden (see p. 44).

The monument to the Roman veteran, Lucius Poblicius.

grew to become the capital of the Roman province of Germania Inferior, and how the town's houses were furnished and decorated. Furnishings from the villa kitchens and dining rooms are exhibited, as well as personal possessions of both men and women, not to mention children's toys. How the Romans and their contemporaries paid tribute to their dead is revealed by sarcophagi, urns, funeral statuary, and grave goods for the deceased, and a reconstructed wagon gives an insight into technical advances in the Roman Empire. The collection of Roman glassware (the largest in the world), much of which was found in Cologne tombs as grave goods, the clay lamps, the frescoes, and the Roman and early medieval jewellery are testaments to the high-quality work of contemporary artisans. Pieces such as the cage cup from around AD 330–340 are particularly worth seeing. The goblet is enclosed in a fine network of gold tracery. Glassware

with playful patterns of different shades or engraved decoration was the trademark of contemporary Cologne glassblowers' workshops.

The museum also has finds from the Palaeolithic, Mesolithic, and Neolithic periods, as well as the Bronze and Iron Age, covering a period from about 100,000 BC to the first century before Christ. Most of the exhibits are from Cologne or the Rhineland, but these are complemented with finds from throughout Europe; of especial note are the clay pots from the Bronze and Iron Ages, and the decorative work from the dresses of Frankish women, although they are not quite as old as the Roman finds.

Several external locations

Several structures nearby are also part of the museum, such as the Praetorium, once the residence of the Roman governor of Germania Inferior, and the mikvah, a ritual bath for women from the medieval Jewish community; both are on display in the Town Hall. The word "mikvah", as used in the Hebrew Bible, means a "collection" – generally, a collection of water. This museum is one of Germany's most famous and most visited and is highly recommended to all visitors, whether amateur or professional historians.

Made of marble, and yet still full of life: a Roman bust of an emperor.

In 2001 the museum moved into its own premises; until then, only a portion of the total holdings had been exhibited, as it had shared a space with the Museum Ludwig. Oswald Maria Ungers was set the challenge of designing a building that would let in indirect light only, because many of the exhibited paintings are highly photosensitive.

INFO

Wallraf-Richartz Museum, Obenmarspforten, Tel. (0221) 22 12 11 19, Tues, Wed, Fri 10.00–18.00, Thurs 10.00–22.00, Sat, Sun 11.00–18.00, U-Bahn to Heumarkt.

Medieval painting

At the heart of Ferdinand Franz Wallraf's collection is the medieval art he found in Cologne's churches and chapels, collected at a time when Napoleon's troops occupied the Rhineland, and monasteries and churches were being dissolved and stripped of their property. The museum currently possesses 290 pictures from Cologne from the period between 1250 and 1550 (of 350 works by this school worldwide). Cologne's painters were often adherents of the so-called "soft style", whereby the Madonna was depicted with a faraway expression

Madonna in the Rose Bower by Stephan Lochner.

and a graceful demeanor. While many of the painters' names are known, the paintings went unsigned, and only a few can be ascribed with any certainty to the greatest artist among them: Stephan Lochner (c. 1400–1451), who painted the *Last Judgement* and *Madonna in the Rose Bower*.

A cube of art

From outside it looks like a bunker, but inside there is a collection of art of the first order: the Wallraf-Richartz Museum – Fondation Corboud has presented this duality to the world since moving into its new building in 2001. The architect, Oswald Mathias Ungers, has created an almost windowless cube, offering ideal exhibition conditions in that most of the paintings displayed here are extremely sensitive to direct light.

Generous collectors

Works of art dating from the 13th to the early 20th century are on display here. The fact that they are to be seen in Cologne is down to the acquisitiveness and generosity of three citizens: Ferdinand Franz Wallraf (1748–1824) was a priest, a doctor of philosophy and of medicine, a professor, and rector of the university who collected art and bequeathed it to the city of Cologne; a merchant, Johann Heinrich Richartz (1759–1861), funded the construction of the first museum building to house the collection; and in March 2001, Gérard J. Corboud, a Swiss entrepreneur born in 1925 and a Cologne resident of long standing, gave his collection of 170 impressionist and pointillist paintings to Cologne on "permanent loan".

These treasures spanning 700 years are displayed in the museum in four sections: the medieval section, with 13th- to 16th-century masterpieces from the Cologne school (see sidebar), the baroque section, the 18th- and 19th-century section, and the Print Room. The masterpieces from the Corboud collection have been integrated thematically. Unfortunately, however, the museum cannot display all the treasures it possesses.

Baroque masterpieces

Displayed thematically and chronologically, works by the Spanish artist Murillo, the great Flemish painter Peter Paul Rubens, and the Dutch genius Rembrandt are to be

Villa in Sevrès by Gabriele Münter. The artist was a member of the "Blue Rider" group, whose pictures she preserved during the Nazi period and World War II.

Rather unprepossessing from the outside, this building is named after two famous art collectors and patrons whose collections have been donated to Cologne or are on permanent loan. The museum specializes in paintings from the 13th to the 20th century.

Jean Renoir, Sewing (1900) by Auguste Renoir.

found in the baroque section. Paintings by Tintoretto and Murillo open the baroque period and are followed by pieces by the Flemish masters Rubens, Jordaens, and Van Dyck, who – well aware of their own importance – reveled in the exposition of opulence. This is a theme continued by the museum today. Three works by Rubens are hung side-by-side: the *Self-Portrait in a Circle of Friends from Mantua*, the *Stigmatization of St Francis*, and *Juno and Argus*. After Rubens, masterpieces from the Golden Age of Dutch painting are displayed: portraits by Rembrandt and Frans Hals hang next to still lifes by Wilhelm and Pieter Claesz, genre paintings by Pieter de Hooch and Jan Steen, and landscapes by Jacob van Ruisdael and Albert Cuyp.

Somewhat unjustly, in previous times Rembrandt's successors were neglected. Today the Wallraf-Richartz Museum exhibits works by Gerrit Dou, Jacob Toorenvliet, and Gerard De Lairesse, who, although inevitably overshadowed by

their illustrious predecessor, had no reason to hide their impressive technical brilliance. Pictures by Canaletto and François Boucher represent the last echoes of the baroque and anticipate the art of coming eras.

The Wallraf-Richartz Museum holds the largest collection of impressionist and post-impressionist masterpieces in Germany. Under the heading "Emerging into the Modern", the 19th-century painting and sculpture section displays famous works by Vincent van Gogh, Claude Monet, and Paul Cézanne, as well as less well-known works by expressionists such as Max Beckmann, Alexei von Javlenski, and Edvard Munch.

A comprehensive drawing collection

The drawing collection comprises 75,000 works, created from the Middle Ages to the early 20th century. There are masterpieces by Leonardo da Vinci and Rembrandt to be admired, and the museum possesses complete sketchbooks by some great artists. Many of the finest artists of European art history are represented in the print section, with woodcuts, copper prints, engravings, and lithography. The baroque department exhibits a rotating exhibition drawn from the print collection.

The legacy of genius: Rembrandt, self-portrait.

When the museum was opened in 1986, after a ten-year period of planning and construction, Cologne was two attractions the richer: an art collection, and a building that immediately enthused the public, exciting both gallery visitors, who appreciated the ideal conditions it created for modern art, and every lover of the Cologne skyline.

INFO
Museum Ludwig, Heinrich-Böll-Platz, Tel. (0221) 22 12 61 65, Tues–Sun 10.00–18.00, every first Fri of the month 10.00–22.00, U-/S-Bahn Dom Hbf.

Pop Art

Pop art grew out of the late 1950s and early 1960s, as a reaction to then-prevalent artistic approaches like the abstract impressionism of Willem de Kooning and Jackson Pollocks's action paintings. Painting and drawing became representational again, even consciously adopting the visual language of advertising.

Jasper Johns and Robert Rauschenberg were the first to explore this genre, followed by Andy Warhol, Claes Oldenburg, George Segal, Roy Lichtenstein, Mel Ramos, Tom Wessel-

Bathtub No. 3 (1963) by Tom Wesselmann.

mann, Jim Dine, Richard Hamilton, and Ronald B. Kitaj. The breakthrough came in 1968 when American pop artists were first exhibited with a flourish at the 4th Documenta show in Kassel. Peter Ludwig bought whole series of works – including pieces by Warhol, Lichtenstein, and Picasso – at the time, later donating them to the Museum Ludwig.

A golden glow in the twilight

When an art-collecting couple, the Ludwigs, donated 350 works of modern art to the city of Cologne in 1976, the town fathers decided to build a new gallery next to the cathedral in which to display them. The winning architects in the ensuing competition were the local team of Peter Busmann and Godfried Haberer. They designed the now-familiar curves of the clinker-built museum with its zinc factory roof, shining golden in the evening sun; the building also provides a home for the Cologne Philharmonic Orch-

estra. Inside, 8,000 sq. m (86,000 square feet) of

exhibition space are given over to the fine arts, including the largest collection of pop art outside the United States. In addition to the first tranche of the donation already mentioned, the Ludwigs gave on permanent loan an extensive collection of Russian avant-garde art from 1906 to 1930 and several hundred works by Pablo Picasso, which have since been donated to the museum in perpetuity. The large expressionist collection of the Cologne lawyer Joseph Haubrich, which once formed part of the modern section of the Wallraf-Richartz Museum, has now been incorporated into the Museum Ludwig, and additional works of contem-

porary art have been and will continue to be acquired.

The Museum Ludwig's collection focuses on five main areas: one of these is pop art (see left). The Haubrich collection includes 200 works, all masterpieces, many of which are from the Bridge ("die Brücke") and the Blue Rider ("Blauer Reiter") groups. Haubrich collected Bridge artists, such as Ernst Ludwig Kirchner, Karl Schmidt-Rottluff, Max Pechstein, and Erich Heckel, as well as Blue Rider works by Franz Marc, August Macke, Wassily Kandinsky, and Alexei von Javlenski, and watercolors by Emil Noldes. Another area is the Russian avant-garde of the second and third decades of the 20th century, including many

works by the suprematist artist Kazimir Malevich

Great art in great spaces. Roy Lichtenstein's *M-Maybe* from 1965 is a key work in pop art, introducing the visual language of comics to art.

MUSEUM LUDWIG

In 1976, Peter and Irene Ludwig, a married couple, donated about 350 works of modern art to the city of Cologne, with a view to building a fitting municipal collection on this foundation. The Museum Ludwig is now one of the best-known contemporary and avant-garde art galleries in Europe, as well as a showcase in which current movements in present-day art can reach the public (see p. 48).

(see p. 48)

Lady in a Green Jacket, a piece by August Macke.

(suprematism was concerned with the supremacy of art over all other aspects of life) and works by El Lissitzky, Nikolai Suetin, Ilya Chashnik, Varvara Stepanova, and Alexander Rodchenko.

Picasso again

Picasso is generally considered a master of classic modernism, and he is exceptionally well represented here. The gallery owns 180 original paintings, bronzes, and ceramics, and a further 730 drawings from all periods of his work, including a sketch of his father he made as an 18-year-old and Musketter and Amor, which he created as an 87-year-old in 1969. The collection also contains cubist masterpieces such as *Woman with Mandolin* (1910), *Harlequin with Folded Hands*, and *Woman with an Artichoke* (1942). Among the drawings, *Suite 347* is of particular note, being a series of 347 pictures illustrating the artist's life.

Only a few museums in Germany have a photograph collection. The Museum Ludwig is one of these, with a collection established in 1980 through the acquisition of the Gruber collection of 887 images to add to its own extensive holdings of photographic work by a number of artists. The museum now has around 10,000 examples of applied photography from advertising and journalism, as well as pieces from both the Russian avant-garde and contemporary photographic art, whose best-known exponent in Cologne is Andreas Gursky. Video art, which has flourished since 1970, is also worthy of mention, and there are works here by Jürgen Klauke, Bruce Nauman, Klaus Rinke, and Richard Serra.

It is interesting to note that the Museum Ludwig also sees a role for itself in curating works from the 20th and 21st centuries, and is thus always at pains to acquire contemporary art not yet represented in its current range of holdings. Certain artists are quite consciously targeted, especially works from the 1960s to the 1990s by, among others, Stephan Balkenhol, Gilbert & George, Julian Schnabel, Robert Mapplethorpe, Robert Rauschenberg, Ulrich Rückriem, and Rosemarie Trockel. Kasper König has been director of the museum since November 2000. His aim is to promote a dialogue between visitors and works of art by making use of the project rooms AC: and DC: and by staging a host of events. He feels the museum should be used rather than visited, believing it belongs to everyone and to no one.

Peter Ludwig, collector and patron of the arts, with a work by Picasso at an exhibition opening in 1993.

CITY WALKS

"Of course Cologne exists, but only as a dream," as Heinrich Böll once said of his home town, meaning that Cologne resists any classification. The city unites so many opposites: the second-oldest conurbation in Germany, and yet a modern metropolis; "holy" Cologne with a UNESCO World Heritage cathedral, a dozen Romanesque churches, and an archbishop, and yet home to the sinful and sensual Carnival. Despite all these apparent contradictions, one thing is clear about Cologne: the hub, the beating heart, the starting point for everything is the Cathedral Church of St Peter und St Maria.

Peters Brauhaus is a typical Cologne bar.

Sights

① Cologne Cathedral
The largest church in Germany and also the largest Gothic cathedral in the world; there is no lack of superlatives for Cologne Cathedral. The symbol and heart of Cologne, and a destination for visitors and pilgrims from all over the world (see pp. 28–41).

② Cathedral Square and Hauptbahnhof
A confusion of voices from every country in the world, of music from every corner of the earth: the Cathedral Square in front of the cathedral is the city's convergence point and rendezvous – not always a thing of beauty, but always lively. The roof over the main station's platforms is 24 m (79 feet) high, in a hall 255 m (837 feet) long and 64 m (211 feet) wide – worth seeing in itself (see p. 82).

③ Hohenzollern Bridge
The Hohenzollern Bridge extends exactly along the axis of the cathedral, almost as if the Prussian kings, under whose aegis the first bridge was built, were seeking to unite early 20th-century enthusiasm for technology with the Middle Ages that created the cathedral. The structure, which is used today

exclusively as a railway bridge, is some 409 m (1,350 feet) long (see p. 82).

④ Römisch-Germanisches Museum
The Römish-Germanisches Museum, built between 1970 and 1974 around a mosaic of Dionysus, which once graced a Roman villa, illustrates everyday life in the Roman town of Colonia Claudia Ara Agrippinensium (see pp. 44, 178).

⑤ Museum Ludwig
A temple to culture of the first order lies hidden under this grey factory roof: the Ludwig collection of modern and contemporary art was founded in 1976 with a donation of 350 works of art. The Cologne Philharmonie and its concert hall are to be found under the same roof.

⑥ Town Hall
The most striking aspect of the Town Hall is its late Gothic tower, decorated with sculptures of 124 venerated Cologne characters. A few of them can be recognized with binoculars, for example Stephan Lochner, Heinrich Böll, and Konrad Adenauer. The high Gothic Hansa Room (14thC.) is also of note, as is the Renaissance loggia (16thC.), which fortunately survived the war (see p. 56).

⑦ Alter Markt (Old Market Square)
Surrounded by several beautiful merchants' houses from bygone centuries, this is the largest square in the Old Town and its focal point. The Jan von Werth fountain, created in 1884, stands in the middle (see p. 58).

⑧ Gross St Martin
Large, powerful, and almost overpowering when seen from the outside; inside, surprisingly delicate and light. Gross St Martin church was built in the middle of the 13th century and its Romanesque architecture already betrays traces of the Gothic period to come (see p. 64).

⑨ Wallraf-Richartz-Museum – Fondation Corboud
The Wallraf-Richartz Museum is one of Germany's great painting collections, principally exhibiting European art from the 13th to the end of the 19th century, including many works by Lochner, Dürer, Rubens, and Renoir (see pp. 70, 180).

⑩ Alt St Alban
This 11th-century church, destroyed in World War II, is a memorial to the dead of both world wars.

⑪ Gürzenich
This is Cologne's largest non-religious Gothic building after the Town Hall. Erected in the 15th century as a festival hall for Cologne's citizens, it still fulfils this purpose today: Carnival balls are held here with all the gaiety you might expect from the Rhineland in full celebration. The building was carefully restored in 1997.

Shopping

① Glasgalerie
This glass-roofed mall in the Maritim Hotel has a unique shopping atmosphere and boasts fashion boutiques for him and her, antique shops, and several restaurants, offering pretty much everything from fine dining to regional cuisine.
Heumarkt 20; Tel. 20 27 0.
www.maritim.de

② Pfeifen Heinrichs
Heinrichs store is a haven for pipe smokers, who will find every smoking requisite here. With 10,000 pipes in stock, they have not only the very best, including 800 pipes by the English luxury brand Dunhill, but also tobacco from all round the world and a range of fine cigars.
Martinstr. 16; Tel. 258 22 01; Mon–Fri 9.00–20.00, Sat 9.00–18.00.

③ Foto Lambertin
Cologne's largest photography store, stocking every camera the amateur photographer could wish for, and almost everything a professional could need, whether for an SLR or a viewfinder. A good selection of second-hand stock, including several rare Leicas.
Wallrafplatz; Tel. 920 79 41; Mon–Fri 9.00–19.00, Sat 9.00–16.00.
www.foto-lambertin.de

④ Montezuma Galerie
Jewellery hand-made by the Navajo, Hopi, Zuni, and Santo Domingo Native Americans from the southwestern United States.
Domkloster 1; Tel. 25 89 96 87; Mon–Fri 9.30-19.00; Sat 10.00-18.00

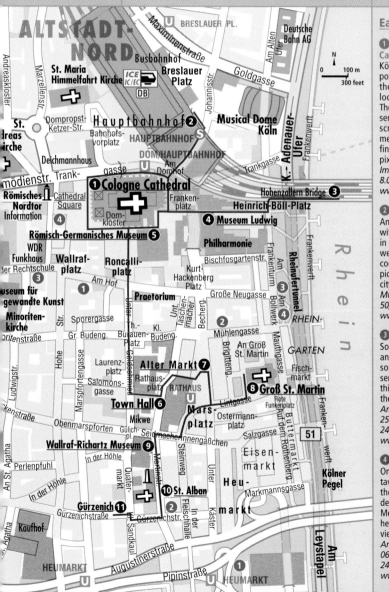

AROUND THE CATHEDRAL AND THE OLD TOWN

Every visit to Cologne begins at the cathedral, but the city has spectacular things to offer in the surrounding area, including unique museums. Please note that the area code for Cologne is **02 21**.

Eating and drinking

❶ Früh by the Cathedral
Kölsch and Hämchen (cooked pork knuckle) right next to the cathedral (Dom), for locals and tourists alike. These Cologne delights are served up in the brewery on scrubbed tables under a medieval vaulted roof, or in fine weather outside by the pixie fountain.
Im Hof 12-14; Tel. 261 32 11; 8.00–24.00, daily.
www.frueh.de

❷ Peters Brauhaus
An enormous brewery pub with nicely fitted-out rooms in a prestigious setting, as well as famously hearty cooking. Among the most picturesque breweries in the city.
Mühlengasse 1; Tel. 257 39 50, 11.00–0.30, daily.
www.peters-brauhaus.de

❸ Em Krützche
Solidly traditional Cologne and Rhineland cooking with some international dishes, served in large portions in this historic bar. The view of the Rhine comes free.
Am Frankenturm 1–3; Tel. 258 08 39; Tues–Sun 10.00–24.00.
www.em-kruetzche.de

❹ Kunibert der Fiese
On the site of a 13th-century tavern, the name (Kunibert the Horrible) is deceptive: delicious Italian and Mediterranean cuisine in the heart of the Old Town, with a view of the Rhine.
Am Bollwerk 1–5; Tel. 258 06 47; Sun–Thurs 8.00–24.00; Fri, Sat 8.00–1.00.
www.kunibertderfiese.de

The 4711 headquarters in the Glockengasse.

Sights

❶ Westdeutscher Rundfunk (WDR)
Cologne and the West German Broadcasting Corporation (WDR) are inseparable. WDR owns several buildings in the heart of the city, although its headquarters are the studios on Wallrafplatz Square, a nice 1950s building with stylish, curved staircases (see p. 118).

❷ Museum für Angewandte Kunst
The rather out-of-the-way Museum of Applied Art houses artisan masterpieces and classics of modern design, as well as clothing style from throughout the world and jewellery dating from the Middle Ages to the present day.

❸ Hohe Strasse
This north-south axis running through the middle of Cologne was laid down by the Romans. In the 1950s it was transformed into one of Germany's first pedestrianized zones, often with crowds of people in the narrow street (see p. 72).

❹ Kolumba
St Columba's church, built in the Middle Ages, was destroyed in World War II; Kolumba, the art museum of the archdiocese of Cologne, was built on its foundations and was finished in 2007. Exhibitions are of Christian art from the Middle Ages to the present, including original statuary from the cathedral.

❺ 4711-Haus
This building in the Glockengasse has Cologne's most famous house number – 4711 – and is where the famous Kölnisch Wasser (Eau de Cologne) comes from. You can buy it here in bottles of every size and shape (see p. 76).

❻ Oper, Schauspielhaus
The opera house and theater complex on Offenbachplatz Square were built in the 1960s. The building's interior is a little more festive than its sober exterior might lead you to expect.

❼ Neumarkt
A square of bustling traffic. The Neumarkt (New Marketplace), laid out as early as the 11th century and before that the middle of the old, post-Roman city, is used today only for bigger public events or for Christmas markets, book sales, or wine fairs; it otherwise serves as a way in to the malls and the pedestrianized zone of the Schildergasse (see p. 72).

❽ St Aposteln
One of Cologne's most beautiful Romanesque churches, with an octagonal west spire over 65 m (214 feet) high, an octagonal tower, a strictly ordered series of roofs and a choir area to the east in the once-fashionable form of a clover leaf, known as a trefoil chancel (see p. 74).

❾ Mittelstrasse, Pfeilstrasse
Closer inspection of these initially unassuming streets reveals them to be Cologne's smartest and most expensive shopping drag: buy fashion, jewellery, accessories, shoes, antiques, and art here.

❿ Brauhaus Päffgen
More than just a brewery pub, this is the apotheosis of Kölsch brewing and drinking. Scrubbed white tables, dark wood panelling on the walls, hearty Rhineland cooking, speedy waiters and, of course, tasty Kölsch, brewed on the premises and poured just when you need it.

⓫ St Gereon
What for many is the most beautiful Romanesque church in Cologne still has architecture fans arguing over which of its features is the most impressive: some rave about the east chancel or the side towers, others about the cupola, where ten supporting columns meet 34 m (112 feet) above the floor. The modern church is the culmination of the work of several centuries and is based on the first sacred building on the site from the late 4th century (see p. 88), dedicated to St Gereon, who was martyred in Cologne.

Shopping

❶ Hoss an der Oper
A traditional delicatessen, owned by the same family for more than 100 years. The range of delights changes weekly and includes numerous home-made treats, such as jams and gelees.
Breite Strasse 25-27; Tel 257 73 93; Tues, Wed, 9.30-18.30, Thurs, Fri 9.30-19.00, Sat 9.00-16.00.
www.hoss-delikatessen.de

FROM WDR TO THE NEUMARKT

Crimes against architecture committed after the destruction of World War II dominate this tour, but nevertheless there are still some real architectural gems to be seen. Please note that the area code for Cologne is **02 21**.

② CCAA-Glasgalerie Köln

The Romans called the town they founded Colonia Claudia Ara Agrippinensium, and these days the CCAA-Glasgalerie sells hand-blown reproductions of original Roman vessels sourced from European museums. They also make glassware in contemporary designs, of course.
Auf dem Berlich 30; Tel 257 61 91; Tues–Fri 10.00–13.00, 14.00–18.00, Sat 10.00–16.00. www.ccaa.de

③ Fahnenfabrik Eleonore Meinel

The Meinel Flag Factory has been producing flags and pennants for 50 years, for customers such as the German national football team, flag-waving bands, members of all sorts of sport and carnival clubs, and even as table decorations. Carnival hats can also be created to your own design.
Hämergasse 16; Tel 257 63 72.

④ Sterck Joh. Jos & Zoon

Incomparable coffee and tea specialists. Coffee and tea from every growing region, English biscuits, and fine pralines to stimulate the senses and tempt those with a sweet tooth, in a charming old store, in a modern shopping street. Sterck also roast their own beans and sell their own blends of coffee.
Neue Langgasse 4; Tel 139 46 34; Mon–Fri 9.30–18.00, Sat 9.00–14.00.

Eating and drinking

① Campi im Funkhaus

Campi is situated right next to the WDR building with a view of Wallrafplatz Square and is thus a popular destination for media types taking a break. Enjoy Italian cuisine and changing specials, with a cool atmosphere.
Wallrafplatz 5; Tel 925 55 55; Mon–Sat 8.00–24.00, Sun, public hols 10.00–23.00. www.campi-im-funkhaus.de

② Holtmann's im MAK

A peaceful oasis in the Museum of Applied Art (MAK), surrounded by the hectic city. Newspapers from around the world, cakes, gourmet coffee, and snacks; eat in the back courtyard in good weather.
*An der Rechtschule; Tel 27 79 88 60; Tues–Sun 11.00–17.00.
www.holtmanns.com*

③ Brauhaus Reissdorf

This is how a brewery is supposed to be run: hearty cooking, long, polished tables, attentive waiting staff.
*Kleiner Griechenmarkt 40; Tel 21 92 54; Sun–Thurs 12.00–24.00, Fri, Sat 12.00–1.00.
www.brauhaus-reissdorf.de*

④ Bieresel

The oldest and largest mussels restaurant in Cologne, it is a traditional dining room with mussels and other dishes, fresh from the sea. Out of the mussels season enjoy Cologne cuisine, such as such as *Himmel und Äd* (blood Wurst with onions, potato, and apple sauce).
*Breite Str. 114; Tel 257 60 90; 11.30–24.00, daily.
www.suenner-brauerei.de*

Powder-puff plant in the botanical gardens.

Sights

❶ St Mariä Himmelfahrt
Cologne is famous for its Romanesque churches and the Gothic cathedral. There are few baroque churches, and this is the most beautiful. Considered the prime example of Jesuit baroque in north-west Germany, building work began here in 1618.

❷ St Ursula
Despite having a Gothic spire, this church dedicated to Cologne's patron saint has a Roman foundation from the 4th century. The impressive Golden Chamber inside is a reliquary chamber from 1643 with over 100 busts filled with relics, and innumerable human bones arranged into various patterns (see p. 86).

❸ Eigelstein
The central axis of the Eigelstein quarter, which runs north from the main station to Ebertplatz Square. An odd mixture of middle-class residential and Turkish influences, with a dash of a Cologne scene that, while not always entirely conventional, is always interesting.

❹ Eigelsteintorburg
This 13th-century gate guarding Cologne's northern exit is one of the few remaining examples of the many gates that once protected the medieval city. A niche in the gate reveals the statue of the "Kölscher Boor", the Cologne farmer, finished in 1885 and erected in 1891 on the occasion of the visit of Emperor William II. The statue is supposed to represent Cologne's loyalty to the empire; indeed, since the late 15th century the city had been foremost in the "Reichsbauer" group, economic hubs that were beholden only to the emperor.

❺ St Kunibert
The northernmost of Cologne's Romanesque churches is also the youngest, built in 1247 at the height of the Gothic period. Nonetheless, the oldest church windows, completed by 1230, are preserved here (see p. 84).

❻ Weckschnapp
A 14th-century defensive tower and once part of the medieval walls, located where the town wall and the Rhine wall met; now integrated into a modern accommodation block.

❼ Bastei
The "bastion" is an important example of 1920s architecture, built on the base of a Prussian tower. The round glazed balcony juts out some 8 m (25 feet) from the plinth.

❽ The Zoo
Opened in 1860, this is Germany's third-oldest zoo and still one of its largest and prettiest, with some 7,000 animals from 700 species accommodated on 20 hectares (50 acres). The elephant park, the rainforest house, where exotic birds can fly about freely, and the aquarium are especially recommended (see p. 114).

❾ Botanical Garden (Forstbotanischer Garten)
The Flora Garden was established in the 19th century as an exotic destination for excursions by the city's better-off classes; a sort of glass palace was soon built, and this is now used as a restaurant and function hall. The hothouses in the botanical gardens next door were built before World War I and have since become part of the delightful Flora Garden (see p. 114).

❿ Rhine Cable Car
The cable car provides perhaps not the best but certainly the most exciting view of the city, and connects the zoo and botanical gardens with the Rhein Park on the other side of the River Rhine. Opened in 1957 for the German National Garden Show, it was the first of its kind in Europe. Each car takes up to four people. The 45-mm (2-inch) thick wire slung between the two pylons is over 900 m (2,900 feet) long.

Shopping

❶ Pfannes und Virnich
Fine pieces in a furniture shop dedicated to the art of living: tables made of rare woods, tasteful lamps, elegant sideboards, and inviting chairs. Everything here is infused with an aesthetic design sense.
Hansaring 88; Tel 992 33 40; Mon–Fri 10.00–18.30, Sat 10.00–15.00.
www.pfannes-virnich.de

THE OLD TOWN (NORTH)

Medieval churches, gates and towers, and a baroque chamber decorated with human bones. Right next to the delights of the zoo and the botanical gardens, with an unusual river crossing courtesy of the Rhine cable car.
Please note that the area code for Cologne is **02 21**.

❷ Markt Altstadt-Nord

Cologne's oldest weekly market has been held on Sudermansplatz Square since 1947, making it Cologne's oldest. It's not so much the goods on offer but the atmosphere that is worth experiencing: Turks and locals rub shoulders and the atmosphere is rough and ready but friendly; the fruit and vegetables are fresh and the household utensils good value. *Sudermanplatz; Tues, Fri 7.00–13.00.*

❸ Aura Holzspielzeug

Germany is well known for the richness of its wood carving tradition and all types of beautifully crafted wooden toys for children of all ages are sold here. The wide range of goods includes non-wooden items for young babies and toddlers. The shop itself is equally beautifully furnished. *Balthasarstr. 48; Tel 120 61 50; Mon–Fri 10.00–14.00, 15.00–15.30, Sat 10.00–13.30.*

❹ Kölner Wein Depot Josef Wittling

A wine merchant's and museum, all under one roof. The building, constructed to echo the gentle slopes of a vineyard has an original garden; in 2003 the roof was planted with more than 700 vines, in an experiment that combines eco-concerns with an unusual marketing ploy. *Amsterdamer Str. 1; Tel 72 75 70; Tues–Fri 8.00–19.00, Sat 8.00–14.00. www.koelnerweindepot.de*

Eating and drinking

❶ Em kölsche Boor

Rustic atmosphere, Rhineland cuisine, and Gaffel-Kölsch beer – a recipe for success, and the brewery has almost 250 years of history behind it. *Eigelstein 121; Tel 13 52 27; daily 10.00–midnight, www.koelscheboor.com*

❷ Café Elefant

A tiny café with great cakes and a reputation to match: a meeting-place popular with strollers, book-lovers, newspaper readers, and anybody else taking it easy. Tasty, home-made blinis, some sweet, some savory. *Weissenburgstr. 50; Tel 73 45 20; daily 10.00–midnight; Sat, Sun, holidays 10.00–20.00*

❸ Bizim

In among the fruit and vegetable markets and the junk shops you'll find the best Turkish restaurant in Germany – or certainly the first to be recognized by Gault Millau. Wonderful fish dishes, nice interior. *Weidengasse 47-49; Tel 13 15 81; daily Tue–Sat midday-15.00, 18.00–23.00*

❹ Wirtshaus Spitz

Right in the middle of the Agnes district, within eyeshot of St Agnes' church, the Spitz bar manages a delicate balancing act, serving Rhineland and Swabian food, including both Rheinischer Sauerbraten (marinated braised beef) and Maultaschen (filled pasta pillows a little like ravioli). *Neusser Strasse 23; Tel 716 69 94; daily 11.00–midnight. www.wirtshaus-spitz.de*

Designer jewellery by Charlotte von Lom.

Sights

❶ St Maria im Kapitol
Cologne's largest Romanesque church, built on the foundations of a Roman temple dedicated to the so-called Capitoline gods, Jupiter, Juno, and Minerva. The modern building was completed in the 11th century, although a predecessor was standing on the site as early as AD 690. The church boasts Germany's first instance of the trefoil or clover-leaf chancel and its benefactor, Ida, abbess of a Benedictine nunnery and scion of the Ottonian imperial house, based the floor plan of the chancel on the Church of the Nativity in Bethlehem (see p. 96).

❷ Overstolzenhaus
The wine trade made the Overstolz family rich in the 13th century, and between 1225 and 1230 they had a prestigious new townhouse constructed, the only residential building from the Romanesque period to survive in Cologne.

❸ St Maria Lyskirchen
A simple pink exterior with a bright interior: built between 1210 and 1220, St Maria Lyskirchen has survived intact; even the frescoes are perfectly preserved. Painted between 1230 and 1270, they depict scenes from the Old and New Testament.

❹ Schokoladenmuseum
The Chocolate Museum tells you all you need to know about growing and processing cocoa beans, although it's not just dry facts and charts; if you have a sweet tooth you are in the right place, as there is plenty to taste, whether in the foyer, with its liquid chocolate fountain, or in the adjoining gift shop (see p. 104).

❺ Deutsches Sport- und Olympiamuseum
The German Sport and Olympics Museum records the history of competitive sports from the ancient Olympics to the economic aspects of professional sport, showing unforgettable highlights, great sports personalities and triumphant victories, as well as bitter defeats (see p. 104).

❻ Bayenturm
The southern end of several kilometres of fortifications situated at the meeting place of the city wall and the Rhine wall, the "Bavarian Tower" is a solid 13th-century bastion, nowadays the home of the FrauenMediaTurm, an archive and information point for the history of the women's emancipation movement.

❼ Rautenstrauch-Joest-Museum
Cologne's own Ethnological Museum is rather cramped, but engaging: it has important collections of Indian art and cultural objects from North and South America, as well as art and artefacts from Africa and Oceania. The museum exists to create respect for non-European cultures. The core of the museum's collection comes from that of Wilhelm Joest, a 19th-century ethnologist, while his sister Adele and her husband donated the purpose-built building.

❽ Severinstorburg
The southernmost of the medieval city gate fortifications, situated on Chlodwigplatz Square since the 12th century. The upper part of the cellar is 12th-century; the rest has since been rebuilt. Function rooms of various sizes are available here for private hire.

❾ St Severin
The "southern cathedral" is a mixture of architectural periods. Several refurbishments and extensions have lent the Romanesque basilica (begun in the 10th century) a Gothic air: the ornamental west façade and spire even look late Gothic. The remains of St Severin are kept here, giving the church its name. The importance of the Carnival in the south of the city has left its mark on the church; in the lower portion of the west façade window there is a tiny carnival clown.

Shopping

❶ Trüffel Ullrich
Sweet heaven in the south of the city: hand-made pralines, delivered weekly from Belgian chocolatiers, and hand-poured chocolate figurines and objects.
Severinstr. 95b; Tel 310 05 38; Mon–Fri 9.30–18.30, Sat 9.30–14.00.
www.trueffel-ullrich.de

❷ Gusto Italiano D.O.C.
Raffaele Juliano covers the whole spectrum of fine Italian delicatessen south of the heart of the city: classic home-made antipasti, more than 20 different kinds of salami, raw and cooked ham, several dozen cheese varieties, fine wines, and spirits.
Severinstr. 18; Tel 331 86 27; Mon–Fri 8.30–18.30, Sat 8.00–14.30.
www.gusto-italiano-doc.de

❸ Charlotte von Lom
Rings, bracelets, necklaces, and earrings: this designer creates the finest jewellery according to her own designs or those of the customer. One-off pieces with clean lines, stripped down to the essentials.
Filzengraben 43; Tel 201 93 89; Tues–Fri 10.00–13.00, 14.30–18.30, Sat 10.00–14.00.
www.charlottevonlom.de

❹ Lelu
A creative dressmaker's, they will alter both to your taste and to your size those clothes you bought and then regretted – and they also design bags.
Im Ferkulum 24-26; Tel 60 60 87 47; Tue–Fri midday–18.30, Sat midday–17.00.
www.le-lu.de

From left: The Chocolate Museum illustrates the history of chocolate; the nave of St Severin's church; sweet things at Trüffel Ullrich's; dining at Maison Blue.

THE OLD TOWN (SOUTH)

Churches, a merchant's house, and the remains of fortifications are witnesses of Cologne's importance in the Middle Ages. The Chocolate Museum has a wealth of information about this "brown gold", and you can even try some. Please note that the area code for Cologne is **02 21**.

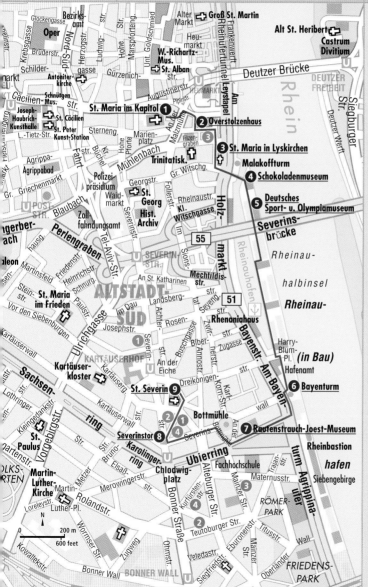

Eating and drinking

① Maison blue
Wooden tables with fresh wild flowers, little lamps, and painted blue walls: fitting surroundings for the French seasonal cuisine celebrated here. A small restaurant with a large kitchen; in summer there are a few tables in the back courtyard.
Im Ferkulum 32; Tel 932 89 96; from 18.30, daily.
www.maisonblue.de

② Litho
More a bar at the front, but at the back there is a light and friendly restaurant. Mediterranean cooking, the freshly prepared fish dishes are recommended. Pick out the marine-dweller of your choice at the ice counter.
Teutoburger Str. 17; Tel 31 75 43; Sun–Thurs 16.00–2.00, Fri, Sat 16.00–3.00.

③ Mainzer Hof
An institution in the south of the city. A nice bar/restaurant with friendly service and regional and seasonal food. Occasional themed culinary evenings. The age group tends to be older but the atmosphere in the evening is usually quite lively. A good place to mix with the locals. Prices are reasonable.
Maternusstr. 18; Tel 31 25 49; from 17.00, daily.
www.mainzerhof-koeln.de

④ Café Zikade
A small café/bistro for vegetarian snacks. The range includes beetroot, rice and noodle salads, wheatcake fritters, and vegetable curry.
Kurfürstenstr. 2a; Tel 31 15 91; Mon–Fri 8.30–20.00, Sat 8.30–19.00.
www.cafezikade.de

Cologne has the most famous skyline of any of Germany's big cities. The cathedral is mainly responsible for this, but the Hohenzollern Bridge and the Romanesque church of Gross St Martin also quickly make an impression.

KEY

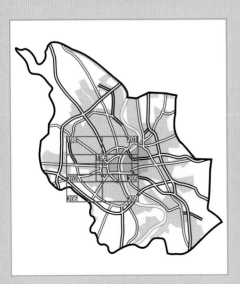

	Motorway (freeway)
	Primary route (arterial road)
	Other road
	Side (local) road
	Footpath
	Pedestrian zone
	Railway (railroad)
	Industrial railway (railroad)
	Regional/Suburban railway (railroad)
	Underground/subway (under construction/planned)
	Car ferry; Passenger ferry

CITY ATLAS

The maps in the City Atlas section give detailed practical information of relevance to tourists to help make your stay more enjoyable. Clear symbols indicate the positions of buildings and monuments of note, facilities and services, public buildings, the transport network, and built-up areas and green spaces (see the key to the maps below).

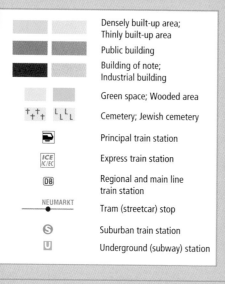

Densely built-up area;
Thinly built-up area

Public building

Building of note;
Industrial building

Green space; Wooded area

Cemetery; Jewish cemetery

Principal train station

Express train station

Regional and main line
train station

NEUMARKT Tram (streetcar) stop

Suburban train station

Underground (subway) station

96 Motorway (freeway) number

2 Primary route (arterial road) number

37 Motorway (freeway) interchange

One-way street

Airport

Stadium

Exhibition hall

Park + Ride

Car park;
Multi-story car park

Bus station

Information

Post office

Hospital

Radio/television tower

Church

Synagogue

Mosque

Column/monument

Theater

Museum

Library

Viewpoint

Port

Cable railway

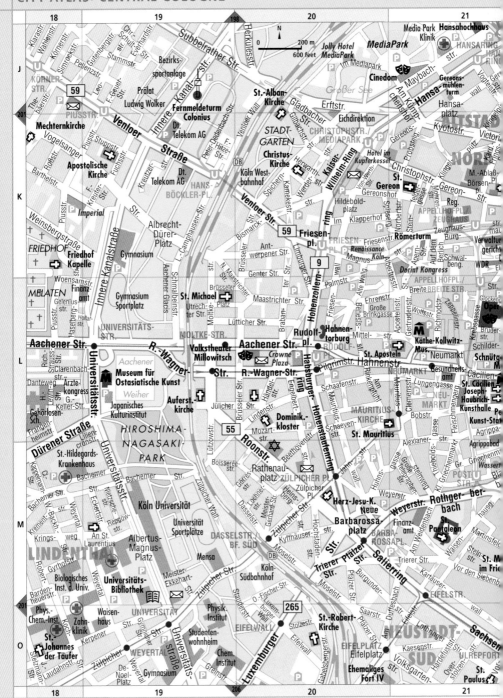

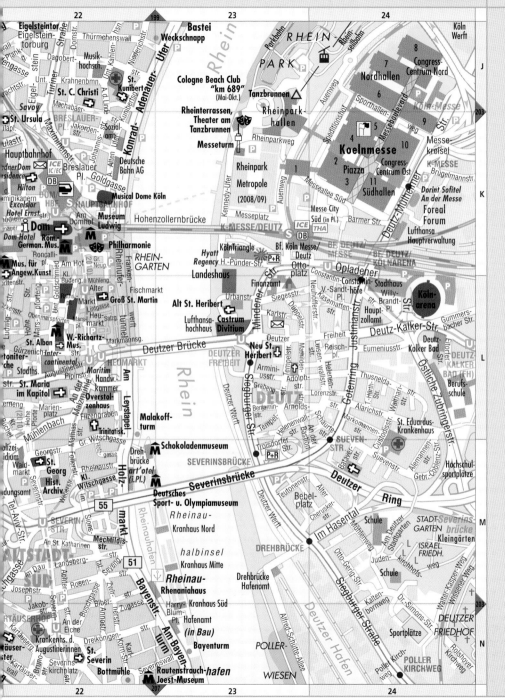

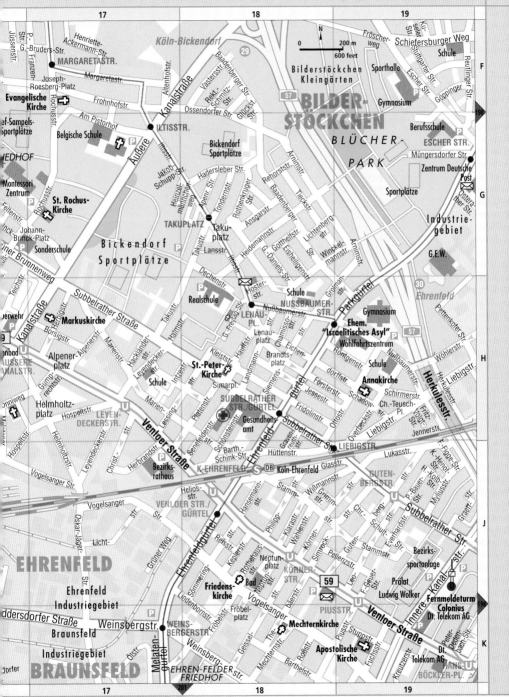

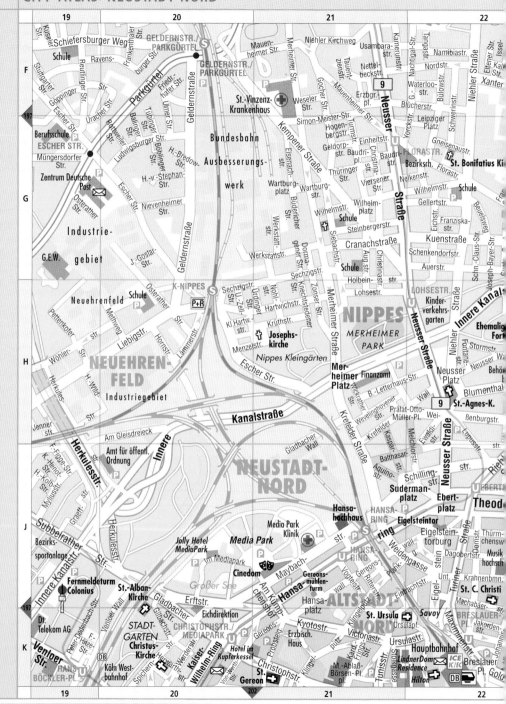

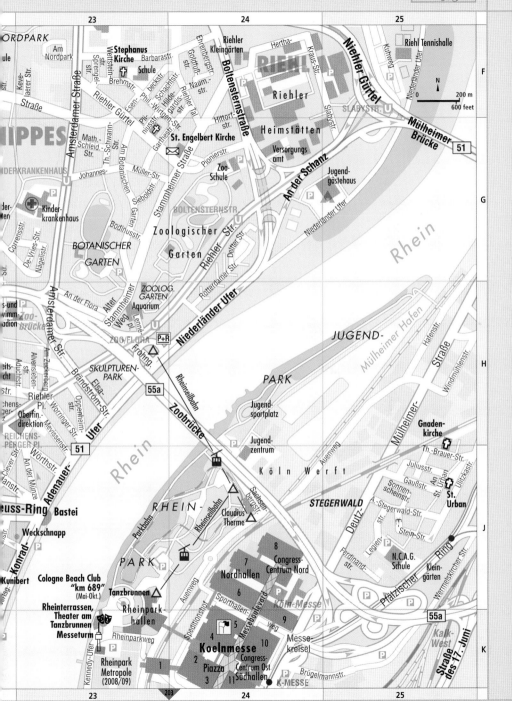

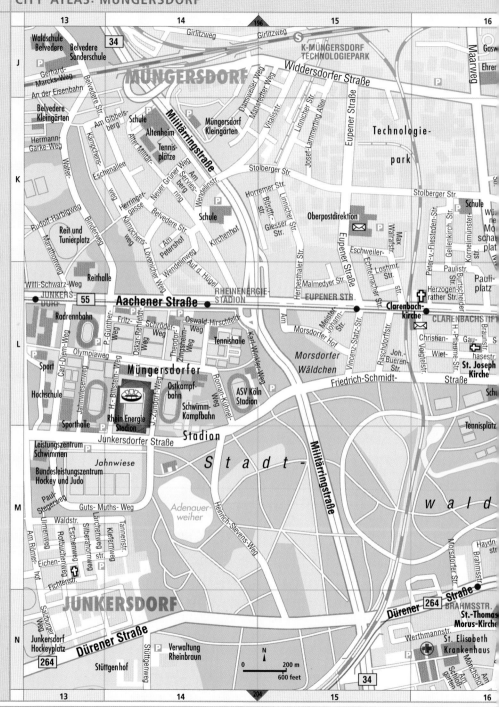

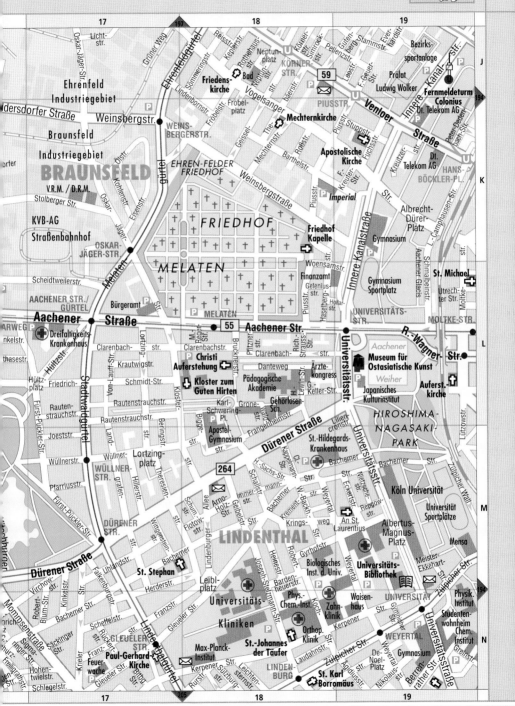

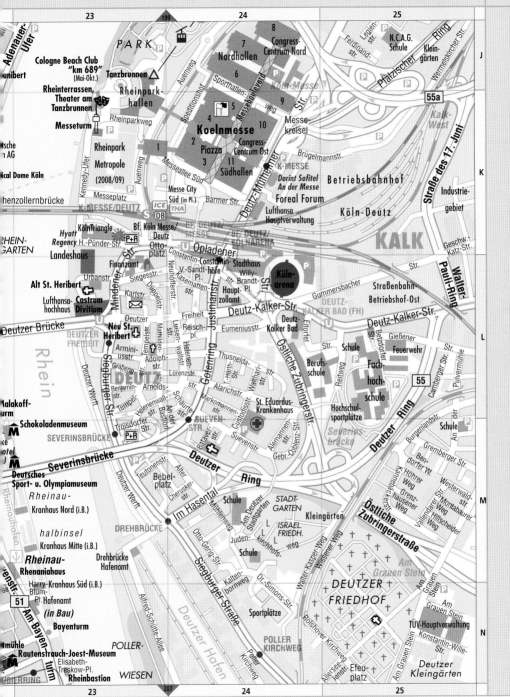

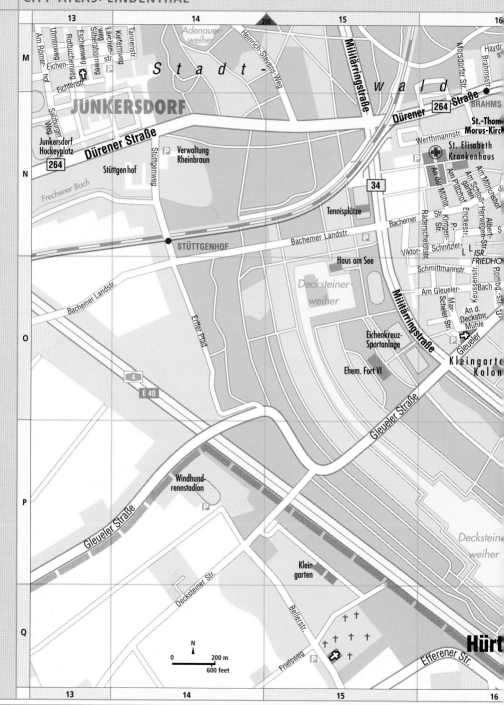

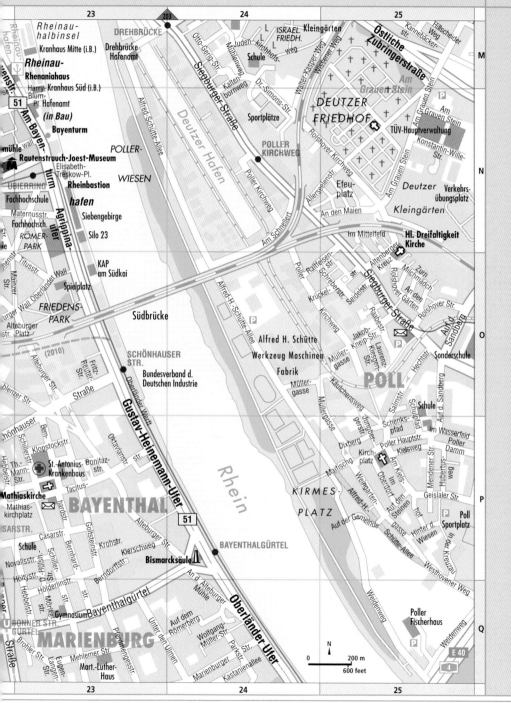

INDEX OF STREETS

Bremsstr.	208	O20
Breniger Str.	208	P20
Breslauer Pl.	200	K22
Briedeler Str.	208	O20
Brohler Str.	209	Q23
Brucknerstr.	203	L18
Brückenstr.	204	L22
Brüderstr.	204	L21
Brügelmannstr.	201	K24
Brüggener Str.	208	Q20
Brühler Str.	208	Q22
Brüsseler Pl.	203	L19
Brüsseler Str.	204	K20
Brunkensteinstr.	207	O17
Brunostr.	204	N22
Buchfinkenweg	198	J15
Büdericher Str.	200	G21
Bülowstr.	200	F22
Büsdorfer Str.	202	K15
Burbach. Str.	208	Q20
Burgenlandstr.	205	L25
Burgmauer	204	K21
Burgunderstr.	204	M20
Burtscheider Str.	202	L16
Buschgasse	204	M22
Bussardweg	198	H15

Cäcilienstr.	204	L21
Cäsarstr.	209	P23
Camberger Str.	205	L25
Carl-Diem-Weg	202	L13
Carl-Schurz-Str.	203	N16
Castellauner Str.	207	O17
Chamissostr.	199	H18
Cheruskerstr.	205	M24
Chlodwigpl.	208	N22
Christian-Gau-Str.	202	L16
Christian-Schult-Str.	199	J19
Christianstr.	199	J17
Christinastr.	200	G21
Christine-Teusch-Pl.	199	H19
Christophstr.	200	K21
Clarenbachstr.	203	L17
Classen-Kappelmann-Str.	203	M18
Clemensstr.	204	L21
Clever Str.	201	J22
Club-Allee	206	P16
Constantinstr.	205	L24
Corrensstr.	201	G22
Cranachstraße	200	G21
Curtiusstr.	207	O18
Custodisstr.	205	L24

Dagobertstr.	200	J22
Daimlerstr.	198	F15
Dansweiler Weg	202	J14
Danteweg	203	L18

Dasselstr.	204	M20
Dauner Str.	207	O18
De-Noel-Pl.	203	N19
De-Vries-Str.	201	G23
Dechenstr.	199	H18
Decksteiner Str.	202	N16
Decksteiner Str.	206	Q14
Delfter Str.	201	G24
Deutz-Kalker-Str.	205	L24
Deutz-Mülheimer-Str.	201	J25
Deutzer Brücke	205	L23
Deutzer Freiheit	205	L23
Deutzer Ring	205	M24
Deutzer Werft	205	L23
Dixberg	209	P25
Dohlenweg	198	H14
Dollendorfer Str.	207	P19
Dompfaffenweg	198	H14
Domstr.	200	J22
Dormagener Str.	200	G21
Dr.-Simons-Str.	205	N24
Drachenfelsstr.	207	P19
Drehbrücke	205	M22
Dreikönigenstr.	205	N22
Droste-Hülshoff-Str.	209	P23
Düppelstr.	205	L23
Dürener Str.	202	N14
Düstemichstr.	208	O19

Ebertpl.	200	J22
Eburonenstr.	209	O22
Echternacher Str.	202	L15
Eckertstr.	203	M19
Edith-Stein-Str.	201	J25
Efeupl.	209	N25
Efferener Str.	206	Q16
Ehrenbergstr.	201	F24
Ehrenfeldgürtel	199	H18
Ehrenstr.	204	L20
Eichelhäherweg	198	H14
Eichendorffstr.	199	H18
Eichenstr.	202	M13
Eichstr.	200	G22
Eifelpl.	204	N20
Eifelstr.	204	N20
Eifelwall	204	N20
Eigelstein	200	J22
Eigelsteintorburg	200	J22
Einhardstr.	207	O19
Einheitstr.	200	G21
Eintrachtstr.	200	J22
Eisenachstr.	200	G21
Eisenstr.	203	K17
Eisheiligenstr.	199	G18
Eitorfer Str.	205	L24
Elisabeth-Treskow-Pl.	205	N23
Elsa-Brändström-Str.	201	H23
Elsaßstr.	208	N22
Elsenborner Str.	203	K16
Elstergasse	204	K21
Eltener Str.	200	F22
Elzstr.	207	P18
Emilstr.	198	F16
Emmastr.	207	O19
Enckestr.	206	N16

Engelbertstr.	204	L20
Ensorstr.	207	Q18
Entenweg	198	H14
Erffer Pfad	206	O14
Erftstr.	200	J20
Erlenweg	198	F16
Ernst-Wilhelm-Nay-Straße	207	N17
Erpeler Str.	207	O19
Erzbergerpl.	200	F21
Eschenallee	202	K14
Eschenweg	202	M13
Escher Str.	199	F19
Eschweilerstr.	202	K15
Esenbeckstr.	201	F23
Eugen-Langen-Str.	209	Q23
Eumeniusstr.	205	L24
Eupener Str.	202	K15
Euskirchener Str.	207	N18
Everhardstr.	199	J19
Ewaldistr.	200	H22

Falkenburgstr.	203	M17
Falkenweg	198	H15
Feltenstr.	199	G16
Ferdinandstr.	201	J25
Fichtenstr.	202	M13
Filzengraben	204	L22
Fischenicher Str.	208	Q20
Flamingoweg	198	H15
Fleischmengergasse	204	L21
Florastr.	200	G22
Flotowstr.	203	M18
Försterstr.	199	H18
Follerstr.	204	M22
Fontanestr.	200	H22
Frangenheimstr.	203	L18
Frankenthaler Str.	200	F20
Frankenwerft	205	L22
Frans-Liszt-Str.	198	H16
Franz-Clouth-Str.	200	G22
Franz-Geuer-Str.	203	J19
Franz-Hitze-Str.	203	K19
Franz-Kreuter-Str.	203	K19
Franz-Marc-Str.	207	Q18
Franziskastr.	200	G22
Franzstr.	203	N17
Frechener Pl.	207	N17
Freiligrathstr.	203	N16
Fridolinstr.	199	H18
Friedenstr.	204	M21
Friedrich-Engels-Str.	207	P18
Friedrich-Schmidt-Str.	202	L15
Friedrichhafer Straße	200	F20
Frielsweg	206	Q15
Friesenpl.	204	K20
Friesenstr.	204	K21
Friesenwall	204	L20
Friesheimer Str.	208	Q20
Fritz-Figge-Str.	199	J19
Fritz-Hecker-Str.	208	Q21
Fritz-Reuter-Str.	209	O23
Fritz-Schröder-Weg	202	L14
Fritz-Voigt-Str.	199	H19
Fröbelpl.	203	K18

Hollerather Str.	207	O18
Holunderweg	198	G16
Holzgasse	204	M22
Holzmarkt	204	M22
Homburger Str.	208	O21
Honnefer Pl.	207	O19
Hornstr.	200	H20
Horremer Str.	202	K15
Hospeltstr.	199	J16
Hosterstr.	199	H18
Hubertusweg	209	P25
Hülchrather Str.	200	H22
Hültzpl.	203	L17
Hültzstr.	203	L17
Hüttenstr.	199	J18
Huhnsgasse	204	M20

Iltisstr.	199	G17
Im Dau	204	M22
Im Hasental	205	M24
Im Klapperhof	204	K20
Im Mediapark	200	J20
Im Mittelfeld	209	N25
Im Oberdorf	209	P25
Im Sionstal	204	M22
Im Wasserfeld	209	P25
Immermannstr.	203	M18
In der Kreuzau	209	P25
Innere Kanalstr.	203	K19
Intzestr.	199	H17
Irmgardstr.	208	P20
Isselburger Str.	200	F22
Ittenberg Str.	207	P19

Jahnstr.	204	M20
Jahnwiesenweg	202	L13
Jakob-Kneip-Str.	209	O25
Jakob-Schupp-Str.	199	G17
Jakob-Zündorf-Weg	202	L14
Jakobstr.	204	N22
Jakordenstr.	200	K22
Jennerstr.	199	H19
Jessestr.	199	H18
Joeststr.	203	M17
Johann-Brinck-Pl.	199	G16
Johann-Brinck-Str.	199	G16
Johann-Bueren-Str.	202	L15
Johann-Heinrich-Pl.	203	N16
Johann-Thomer-Str.	198	F15
Johannes-Müller-Str.	201	G23
Johannisstr.	200	K22
Josef-Esser-Pl.	198	G16
Josef-Hamacher-Pl.	198	H13
Josef-Lammerting Allee	202	K15
Joseph-Bayer-Str.	200	G22
Joseph-Roesberg-Pl.	199	F17
Joseph-Stelzmann-Str.	203	N18

Josephstr.	204	M22
Judenkirchhofsweg	205	M24
Jülicher Str.	204	L19
Jünkerather Str.	207	O18
Jüssenstr.	199	F16
Julio-Goslar-Str.	200	G20
Juliusstr.	201	J25
Jungbergerstr.	209	P25
Junkersdorfer Str.	202	M14
Justinianstr.	205	L24

Kämpchensweg	202	K14
Kaesenstr.	204	N21
Käulchensweg	209	O25
Kaiser-Wilhelm-Ring	200	K20
Kalkarer Str.	200	F22
Kalscheurer Weg	208	Q20
Kaltenbornweg	205	M24
Kamekestr.	204	K20
Kamerunstr.	200	F21
Kannebäckerstr.	205	M25
Kardinal-Frings-Str.	200	K21
Karl-Begas-Str.	207	Q19
Karl-Benz-Str.	198	F15
Karl-Bosch-Str.	198	F15
Karl-Korn-Str.	205	N22
Karl-Schwering-Pl.	203	L18
Karl-Winkler-Weg	202	L14
Karlstr.	205	L23
Karolingerring	208	N22
Kartäusergasse	204	N22
Kartäuserwall	204	M21
Kasemattenstr.	205	L24
Kasparstr.	200	J21
Kastanienallee	209	Q24
Katharina-Henot-Str.	199	J19
Kempener Str.	200	G21
Kempfelder Str.	207	O17
Kennedy-Ufer	201	K23
Keplerstr.	203	J18
Kermeterstr.	207	N17
Kerpener Str.	203	N18
Keussenstr.	206	O16
Kevelaerer Str.	201	F23
Kiebitzweg	198	H14
Kiefernweg	202	M14
Kielsweg	209	P25
Kierberger Str.	208	P21
Kinkelstr.	203	N17
Kirchberger Str.	207	O17
Kirchenhof	202	K14
Kirchpl.	209	P25
Kitschburger Str.	202	M16
Klarastr.	199	J18
Kleiberweg	198	H14
Kleine Budengasse	204	L22
Kleine Griechenmarkt	204	M21
Kleine Hartwichstr.	200	H20
Kleine Witschgasse	204	M22
Kleingedankstr.	204	N21
Kleiststr.	199	H18
Klerschweg	209	P23
Klettenberggürtel	207	P19
Klingelpütz	200	K21
Klopstockstr.	209	P23

Klosterstr.	203	M17
Klüsserather Straße	208	P20
Knapsacker Str.	208	Q20
Knechtstedener Str.	200	H21
Koblenzer Str.	209	O22
Königswinterstr.	207	O19
Körnerstr.	199	J18
Kohlenstr.	203	K17
Kolibriweg	198	H13
Kolkrabenweg	198	G14
Komödienstr.	204	K21
Konrad-Adenauer-Ufer	201	J23
Konradstr.	207	N19
Konstantin-Wille-Str.	205	N25
Koppensteinstr.	207	O16
Kornelimünsterstr.	202	K16
Kottenforststr.	208	P20
Kowallekstr.	208	O21
Krähenweg	198	H14
Kranichweg	198	H14
Krautwigstr.	203	L17
Krebsgasse	204	L21
Krefelder Str.	200	H21
Krefelder Wall	200	H21
Krementstr.	203	M18
Kretzerstr.	201	F22
Kreutzerstr.	203	K19
Kreuznacher Str.	208	P21
Krieler Str.	203	N17
Kringsweg	203	M18
Kröver Str.	208	O20
Krohstr.	209	P23
Kronenburger Str.	207	N17
Krückelstr.	209	O25
Krüthstr.	200	H21
Krummer Büchel	204	L22
Kuckucksweg	198	H15
Kuenstraße	200	G22
Kuhweg	201	F25
Kunibertsgasse	201	J22
Kurfürstenstr.	208	N22
Kuseler Str.	199	F19
Kyffhäuserstr.	204	M20
Kyllburger Str.	207	O18
Kyllstr.	209	O22
Kyotostr.	200	K21

Lämmerstr.	200	H20
Lärchenweg	202	M13
Landgrafenstr.	203	M17
Landmannstr.	199	H18
Landsbergstr.	204	M22
Landskronstr.	208	P21
Lansstr.	199	G18
Laudahnstr.	203	N18
Laurenz-Kiesgen-Str.	209	O25
Lechenicher Str.	207	N18
Legienstr.	201	J25
Lehmbruckstr.	207	Q18
Leiblpl.	203	M18
Leichtensternstr.	203	N18
Leichweg	208	Q21
Leipziger Pl.	200	G22

Oberländer Werft	209	O23
Oberpleiser Str.	207	Q19
Ölbergstr.	207	P19
Ölstr.	203	K17
Östliche Zubringerstr.	205	L24
Ohmstr.	208	O22
Oktavianstr.	209	P23
Olefstr.	207	O18
Olympiaweg	202	L14
Opladener Str.	205	L24
Oppenheimstr.	201	H23
Oskar-Jäger-Str.	203	J17
Oskar-Rehfeldt-Weg	202	L14
Ossendorfer Str.	199	G18
Ossendorfer Weg	198	F15
Osterather Str.	199	G19
Oswald-Hirschfeld-Weg	202	L14
Otto-Fischer-Str.	204	M20
Otto-Gerig-Str.	205	M24
Ottopl.	205	K23
Ottostr.	199	H19
Overbeckstr.	199	H19
Overstolzenstr.	204	N21
Palanterstr.	203	N19

Palmstr.	204	L20
Parkgürtel	200	F20
Parkstr.	209	Q24
Paul-Schallück-Str.	208	N20
Paul-Stegerweg	202	M13
Paulipl.	202	L16
Paulistr.	202	L16
Paulstr.	204	M21
Pellenzstr.	203	J19
Perlengraben	204	M21
Peter-Bauer-Str.	199	J19
Peter-Dedenbach-Str.	203	K19
Peter-Franzen-Str.	199	F17
Peter-Günther-Weg	202	L14
Peter-Kintgen-Str.	206	N16
Peter-von-Fliesteden-Str.	202	K16
Petersbergstr.	207	O19
Pettenkofer Str.	199	H19
Pfälzer Str.	204	M20
Pfälzischer Ring	201	J25
Pfarriusstr.	203	M17
Pferdmengesstr.	209	Q23
Pfitznerstr.	203	L18
Philipp-Wirtgen-Str.	201	F23
Philippstr.	199	J18
Pilgrimstr.	204	L20
Pionierstr.	201	G24
Pipinstr.	204	L22
Pirolweg	198	H14
Piusstr.	203	K19
Plankgasse	200	J21
Platanenweg	198	G16
Platenstr.	199	H18
Pliniusstr.	201	G23
Pohligstr.	208	O20
Poller Damm	209	P25
Poller Hauptstr.	209	P25

Poller Kirchweg	209	N24
Prälat-Otto-Müller-Pl.	200	H22
Privatstr.	198	H16
Probsteigasse	200	K21

Raabestr.	209	O25
Raderberger Str.	208	P22
Raderberggürtel	208	Q22
Raderthaler Str.	208	Q21
Raderthalgürtel	208	Q21
Räderscheidtstr.	206	N16
Raitfeisenstr.	209	O25
Raschdorffstr.	202	L15
Rathauspl.	204	L22
Rathenaupl.	204	M20
Rautenstrauchstr.	203	L17
Ravensburger Str.	200	F20
Redwitzstr.	207	N19
Rehorststr.	199	G18
Reichenspergerpl.	201	H22
Reiherweg	198	G14
Reischpl.	205	L24
Reisstr.	203	J18
Reitweg	205	L25
Rektor-Schmitz-Str.	199	F18
Remigiusstr.	207	N19
Rennebergstr.	207	N19
Repgowstr.	203	M19
Reutlinger Str.	199	F19
Rheinaustr.	204	M22
Rheinparkweg	201	K23
Rheinsteinstr.	208	P22
Rheinufertunnel	204	L22
Rhöndorfer Str.	208	O20
Richard-Strauss-Str.	203	L18
Richard-Wagner-Str.	203	L19
Richmodstr.	204	L21
Riehler Gürtel	201	F23
Riehler Pl.	201	H23
Riehler Str.	201	G24
Riehler Tal	201	F24
Ritterstr.	200	J21
Robert-Blum-Str.	203	N17
Robert-Koch-Str.	203	N18
Robert-Seuffert-Str.	207	Q18
Rochusstr.	199	F17
Rodderbergstr.	207	P18
Röntgenstr.	199	H19
Roisdorfer Str.	208	Q20
Rolandstr.	208	O22
Rolandswerther Str.	207	P18
Rolshover Kirchweg	205	N25
Rolshover Str.	209	O25
Roman-Kühnel-Weg	202	L14
Rombergstr.	206	O16
Roncallipl.	204	K22
Roonstr.	204	M20
Rosenstr.	204	M22
Rosenzweigweg	208	P20
Roßstr.	203	K18
Rotbuchenweg	202	M13
Rotdornweg	198	G16
Rothehausstr.	203	J18
Rothenkruger Str.	199	G18
Rothgerberbach	204	M21

Rotkehlchenweg	198	H15
Rotschwänzchenweg	198	H14
Rotterdamer Str.	201	H24
Rottweiler Str.	200	G20
Rudolf-Amelunxen-Str.	208	N20
Rudolf-Harbigweg	202	K13
Rudolfpl.	204	L20
Rückertstr.	203	N17
Rupprechtstr.	207	N18
Rurstr.	207	N17

S.-Hartmann-Str.	208	O20
Saarstr.	204	N20
Sachsenbergstr.	201	J24
Sachsenring	204	N21
Säckinger Str.	203	N17
Salierring	204	M21
Salmstr.	209	O25
Salzburger Weg	202	N13
Salzgasse	204	L22
Sandweg	198	F16
Schaafenstr.	204	L20
Schachtstr.	201	F23
Schadowstr.	199	H19
Schaevenstr.	204	L20
Schaffhausener Str.	206	N16
Schallstr.	203	M18
Schaurtestr.	205	L24
Scheffelstr.	203	N17
Scheidtweilerstr.	203	L17
Schenkendorfstr.	200	G22
Schenkspfad	209	P25
Scherfginstr.	207	P18
Schiefersburger Weg	200	F19
Schildergasse	204	L21
Schillerstr.	209	P23
Schillingstr.	200	J22
Schinkelstr.	203	L16
Schirmerstr.	199	H19
Schlegelstr.	203	N17
Schlehdornweg	198	G16
Schleidener Str.	207	N18
Schmalbeinstr.	203	L19
Schmitbergstr.	207	O17
Schmittmannstr.	206	O16
Schneider-Claus-Str.	200	G22
Schnurgasse	204	M21
Schönhauser Str.	209	O23
Schönsteinstr.	199	H18
Schreberstr.	209	O25
Schulpfad	209	P25
Schumacherstr.	203	M18
Schwalbacher Str.	208	P21
Schwalbengasse	204	K21
Schweinstr.	200	F22
Sechtemer Str.	208	O22
Sechzigstr.	200	G21
Sedanstr.	201	J22
Seeadlerweg	198	F14
Seidelstr.	209	O25
Senefelderstr.	199	H18
Severinsbrücke	205	M23
Severinskirchpl.	204	N22
Severinstr.	204	M22
Severinswall	205	N22

INDEX OF KEY PEOPLE AND PLACES, WITH WEBSITES

Picture credits

Abbreviations

AKG = Archiv für Kunst und Geschichte
BB = Bilderberg
L = Laif
Schapo = Schapowalow
Mohn = Mohnheim

t. = top, m. = middle, b. = bottom, l. = left,
r. = right

Cover front: large image: age fotostock/
Look-foto München; image t.: L/Hoff-
mann, image m.: BB/Sackermann;
image b.: BB ; Cover reverse t.: L/Linke;
m.: AKG; b.: L/Zanettini; p.1: L/Linke;
p.2/3: BB; p.4/5: L/Linke; p.6/7: L/Hoff-
mann; p.8/9: BB; p.10 l.: AKG; p.10 t. 1:
L/Ogando; p.10. 2: L/Klein; p.11 o:
BB/Sackermann; p.10 l.: Otto; p.10. r.:
AKG; p.12 l.: AKG; p.12 r.: AKG; p.12 t.
1: L/Klein; p.12 t. 1: AKG; p.12 b.: AKG;
p.13 t. l.: BB/Sackermann; p.13 t. r.:
Mohn; p.13 l.: BB/Sackermann; p.14 t. l.:
AKG; p.14 t. r.: AKG; p.14 l.: AKG; p.14 r.:
Artur; p.15 t. l.: BB/Sackermann; p.15 t.
r.: AKG; p.15 l.: AKG; p.15 r.: AKG; p.16 t.
l.: AKG; p.16 t. m.: AKG; p.16 t. r.: AKG;
p.16/17: AKG; p.17: AKG; p.18 t.: AKG;
p.18 b.l.: AKG; p.18 b.r.: BB/Sackermann;
p.19 t. l.: AKG; p.19 l.: AKG; p.19 t. r.:
AKG; p.19 b. r.: AKG; p.20 t. l.: AKG; p.20
t. r.: C/Bettmann; p.20 b.: L/Hollandse
Hogte; p.21 t. l.: C/Hulton-Deutsch; p.21
l. m.: AKG; p.21 b. l.: C/Hulton-Deutsch;
p.21 r.: C/Hulton-Deutsch; p.22 t. l.:AKG;
p.22 t. 2: AKG; p.22 t. 3: AKG; p.22 t. 4:
AKG; p.22 t. l.: Kneffel; p.22 b. l.: vario;
p.22 m. t.: artur; p.22 b. r.: artur; p.23 t.
1: AKG; p.23 t. 2: images; p.23 t. 3: vario;
p.23 t.: AKG; p.24/25: Stark; p.28 t. 1:
L/Klein; p.28 l.: BB/Sackermann; p.28/29:
L/Klein; p.28 b.l.: BB/Sackermann; p.29
t. r.: BB; p.30 t.: Mohn; p.30/31: Mohn;
p.31 b.l.: BB/Grames; p.31 m. l.: L/Specht;
p.31 b.l.: BB/Sackermann; p.31 r.: Mohn;
p.32 t. l.: L/Linke; p.32 t. r.: BB; p.32: BB;
p.32/33: L/Linke; p.33: Mohn/Lord; p.34
t.: Visum; p.34 t. l.: Visum; p.34 l. m.: Visum; p.34 b. l.: L/Specht; p.34/35: AKG;
p.36 t. l.: AKG; p.36 t. r.: AKG; p.36/37:
BB; p.36 l.: AKG; p.36 l.: AKG; p.36 r.:
AKG; p.37:AKG; p.38 t. l.: L/Specht; p.40
t. m.: L/Specht; p.40 t. r.: L/Ogando; 40 b.:
L/Ogando; p.40/41: L/Kreuels; p.41 t. :
L/Kreuels; p.41 m.: L/Kreuels; p.41 b.:

L/Kreuels; p.42 b.l.: BB/Sackermann;
p.42 b. m.: BB/Ginter; p.42 o: Dom Hotel
Cologne; p.42/43: L/Heidorn; p.42 b. m.:
L/Linke; p.43 r: Getty; p.44 t. l.: BB; p.44
t. r.:W. Otto; p.44/45: L/Huber; p.46 t. l.:
BB/Sackermann; p.46: L/Linke; p.46 t. l.:
Artur; p.46 t. r.: Mohn; p.46/47: L/Linke;
p.46 b.: BB; p.47 t. l.: BB/Sackermann;
p.47: BB; p.48 t. l.: Getty; p.48/49:
L/Klein; p.49 t. l.: L/Linke; p.49 t. r.:
BB/Sackermann; p.50 t.1: AKG; p.50 t. 2:
AKG; p.50 t. 3: AKG; p.50 t. 4: Visum;
p.50/51: L/Klein; p.51 t. l.: L/Linke; p.51 l.
m.: BB/Ginter; p.51 b. l.: BB; p.52/53:
L/Linke; p.56 t.: alimdi; p.56/57: L/Klein;
p.57 t.: L/Klein; p.57 b.: L/Klein; p.58 t.:
Schapo; p.58.l.: L/Klein; p.58/59:
L/Ogando; p.60 t. l.: L/Ogando; p.60 t. r.:
L/Linke; p.60 l.: BB; p.60/61: L/Linke; p.61
r.: BB; p.62 t. l.: L/Huber; p.62 t. r.: L/Hu-
ber; p.62 t. 1.: L/Huber; p.62 l. 2.: L/Tuere-
mis; p.62 l. 3: BB; p.62 l. 4: BB; p.62 l. 5:
Schapo; p.62/63: L/Hoffmann p.63 t. 1:
L/Linke; p.63 t. 2: L/Linke; p.63 t. 3: L/Tue-
remis; p.63 t. 4: Version; p.63 t. 5: L/Za-
nettini; p.64 l.: GlobalGuest Germany
GmbH & Co.KG; p.64 r.1.: alimdi/Szoe-
nyi; p.64/65: L/Linke; p.65 t. r.: L/Klein;
p.65 r.: Artur; p.66 t. l.: L/Ogando; p.66 t.
r.: L; p.66 l.: L/Jung; p.66/67: L/Zanettini;
p.67 t. l.: L/Linke; p.67 t. r.1: L/Specht; p.67
t. 2: L/Jung; p.67 t. 3: L/Jung; p.67 t. 4:
L/Jung; p.68 t.: L/Klein; p.68 l.: BB/Sacker-
mann; p.68/69: L/Linke; p.68 t. l.: AKG;
p.70. 1.: Artur; p.70.2.r.: Artur; p.70/71:
BB/Ginter; p.71 t.: L/Linke; p.71 b.: L/Lin-
ke; p.72 t. l.: BB/Sackermann; p.72 t. r.:
L/Specht; p.72 l.: p-a/dpa; p.72/73: p-
a/dpa; p.74 t. l.: Mohn; p.74 t. r.: Mohn;
p.74 l.: Mohn; p.74/75: BB/Sackermann;
p.75 r.: BB; p.76 t. l.: TV-yesterday; p.76 t.
m.: TV-yesterday; p.76 t. r.: TV-yesterday;
p.76/77: BB/Sackermann; p.77 b.l.: L/Lin-
ke; p.77 b. m.: BB/Sackermann; p.77 b. r.:
L; p.78/79: BB; p.82 t. l.: BB/Schmid; p.82
b.l.: BB/Sackermann; p.82 b. r.: BB/Sac-
kermann; p.82/83: BB/Sackermann; p.84
t.: L/Linke; p.84 l.: Mohn; p.84/85:
BB/Sackermann; p.85 r.: Mohn; p.85 b.l.:
Mohn; p.85 b.r.: Mohn; p.85 b.r.: Mohn;
p.86 t.: Mohn; p.86/87: BB/Sackermann;
p.88 t.: BB; p.88 b.l.: BB; p.88/89: Zielske; p.89 r.: L/Gaasterland; p.90 t. l.: BB;
p.90 t. r.: BB; p.90: artur; p.90/91: BB/Sac-
kermann; p.91: Mohn; p.92/93: L/Klein;
p.96 t. l.: Mohn; p.96 t. r.: Mohn; p.96/97:
BB; p.96 u.l. : Stadtkonservator Köln,
p.97: BB/Sackermann; p.98 t. l.: Mohn;
p.98 t. r.: Mohn; p.98 l.: Mohn; p.98/99:

Mohn; p.99: Mohn; p.100 t.: Mohn;
p.100/101: BB; p.101: BB/Sackermann;
p.102 t.: Mohn; p.102 u.l.: Mohn;
p.102/103: Mohn; p.103 r.: Mohn; p.104
t.: L/Elleringmann; p.104 1.: L/Elering-
mann, p.104 2.: DFA;, p.104 3.: L/Scho-
ne; p.104 4: BB/Sackermann;
p.104/105: BB/ Sackermann; p.106 t.:
BB/Sackermann; p.106/107: L/Linke;
p.108/109: L/Specht; p.112 t.: Cölner
Hofbräu P. Josef Früh KG; p.112 b.l.:
LKlein; p.112 b.r.: L/Linke; p.112 l.: L/Lin-
ke; p.112/113: L/Linke; p.113 r: Mohn;
p.114 t. l.: Zegers; p.114 t. r.: Okapia;
p.114/115: BB/Sackermann; p.114 b.l.:
f1online; p.114 b.r.: BB/Sackermann;
p.115 1: Westend61; p.115 2: Cover-
Spot/Lauter; p.115 3: f1online; p.115
4:images/ Siegmann; p.116 t.: Nicole
Breukmann. p.116/117: BB/Sacker-
mann; p.117 t.: L/Kost p.117 r.: BB; p.118
t.: L/Baatz; p.118 l.: L/Gaasterland; p.118
t. 1: L/Ogando; p.118 r. 2: L/Ogando;
p.118 r. 3: L/Rabsch; p.118 r. 4: L/Baatz;
p.119 l. 1: L/Linke; p.119 l. 2: L/Tjaden;
p.119 l. 3: L/Zelck; p.119 l. 4: L/Baatz;
p.119 l. 5: L/Linke; p.119 r.: L/Rabsch;
p.120 t. l.: BB/Sackermann; p.120 t. r.: BB;
p.120 l.: BB; p.120 b.l.: BB/Steinhilber;
p.120 b.r.: f1online; p.120 M: BB; p.121:
BB; p.122 l.: Hellers Brauerei; p.122 b.l.:
BB/Enders; S.122 b. m.: BB/Enders; p.122
l.: L/Schoene; p.122/123: L/Futh; p.122 r.
1: L/Specht; p.122 r. 2: L/Specht; p.122 r.
3: L/Specht; p.122 r. 4: L/Enker; p.124 t. l.:
BB/artur; p.125 u.l.: Kraft; p.125 b.r.: Co-
verSpot; p.124/125: C/Ruesche; p.126 t.:
AKG; p.126/ 127: C/Bassouls; p.127 t.:
p-a/Wellershof; p.127 b.r.: p-a/Scheide-
mann; p.128/129: BB/Sackermann;
p.132 t.: L/Linke; p.132/133: BB/ Letz;
p.133 t.: L/Linke; p.133 b.: BB/Fischer;
p.134 r.: L/Klein; p.134/ 135: L/Klein;
p.135: BB/Sackermann; p.136 t.: Schiefer; p.136/137: BB/ Sackermann; p.136
b.l.: L/Specht; p.136 b.r.: BB; p.138 t. l.:
BB; p.138 t. r.: BB; p.138 b.l.: BB; p.138
b.r.: BB; p.138/139: BB/Sackermann;
p.139 r. 1: Schiefer; p.139 r. 2: BB/Sacker-
mann; p.139 r. 3: BB; p.139 r. 4: L/Kruell;
p.139 r. 5: BB; p. 139 r. 6: christoph-
papsch; p.139 r.: L/Kruell; p.140 t. l.:
C/Gambarini; p.140 t. r.: C/Cartstensen;
p.140 l.: CoverSport/Lauer; p.140/141:
L/Linke; p.142 t. l.: L/Specht; p.142 l.:
L/Gollhardt&Wieland; p.142/143: L/Za-
nettini; p.144/145: BB/Sackermann;
p.148 t.: BB/Sackermann; p.148/149: BB;
p.149 r.: BB/Sackermann; p.150/151:

Zielske; p.150 t. l.: Mohn; p.150 t. r.:
Mohn; p.153 b.l.: Mohn; p.153 b. m.:
Mohn; p.152 t. r.: Mohn; p.152 t.l.:
BB/Sackermann; p.152/ 153: Mohn;
p.153: Mohn; p.154 t. l.: BB/Sackermann;
p.154 l. 1: BB/Sackermann; p.154/155:
BB/Sackermann; p.156/157: BB/
Schmidt; S.156 t. b.r. :BB/Ginter; p.158/
159: Getty; p.160 t. 1: BB; p.160 t. 2: Version; p.160 t. 3: Schapo; p.160 t. 4: Getty; p.160 m.: L/Getty; p.160 b.:
Visum/Bruch; p.161 t.: L/Klein; p.161 m.:
L/Linke; p.161 b.: BB/Sackermann; p.162
t. 1: L/Klein; p.162 t. 2: BB/Sackermann;
p.162 t. 3: L/Linke; p.162 t. 4: L/Ogando;
p.162 m.: L/Ogando; p.162 b.: L/Gott-
hardt; p.163 t. l.: L; p.163 m.: Weinhaus
Brungs; p.163 b.: artur/ Schwager; p.164
t. 1: L/Linke; p.164 t. 2: BB; p.164 t. 3: BB;
p.165: BB/Sackermann; p.166 1: BB/Sac-
kermann; p.166 2: Zielske; p.166 3: Excelsior Ernst; p.167: Fifi Choo; p.168 1:
L/Klein; p.168 2: L/Elleringmann; p.168
3: L/Elleringmann; p.168 4: DFA; p.168 5:
L/Klein; p.169: Monheim; p.170 1:
BB/Sackermann; p.170 2: L/Linke; p.170
3: L/Linke; p.170 4: L/Specht; p.171: Artur; p.172 1: Schiefer; p.172 2: BB; p.172
3: L/Linke; p.173: L/Gollhardt&Wieland;
p.174 1: Zielske; p.174 2: BB/Sacker-
mann; p.174 3: BB/Sackermann; p.175:
BB/ Ginter; p.176/177: L/Hemis; p.178 t.:
Look/TerraVista; p. 178 l.: Arco/Svarc;
p.178 b.: Otto; p.179 t.: Otto; p.179 m.:
Otto; p.179 r: version; p.180 t.: AKG;
p.180 l.: AKG; p.180 b.: AKG; p.181 t.:
christoph-pabsch; p.181 m.: AKG; p.181
t.: Bridgeman; p.182 t.: Getty; p.182 l.:
AKG; p.182 b.: AKG; p.183 t.:
Visum/Franken; p.183 m.: bridgeman;
p.183 r.: AKG; p.184/185: L/Klein; p.186
t. 1: BB; p.186 t. 2: BB/Sackermann;
p.186 t. 3: Engelelf p.186 b.: Peters Brauhaus; p.187: Cölner Hofbräuhaus P. Josef Früh KG; p.188 t. 1: BB; p.188 t. 2:
Hoss Delikatessen; p.188 t. 3: p-a/dpa;
p.188 b.: BB/Sackermann; p.189: Holtmann's; p.190 t. 1: Zegers; p.190 t. 2:
Monheim; p.190 t. 3: Kölner Wein Depot;
p.190 b.: BB; p.191 : Wirtshaus Spitz;
p.192 t. 1: BB/Sackermann; p.192 t. 2:
Monheim; p.192 t. 3: Trüffel Ullrich;
p.192 b.: Charlotte vom Lom; p.193:
Maison Blue.

© for illustrations on pp. 180 b., 182 l.,
182 b.and 183 r.: VG Bild-Kunst, Bonn
2008, for image on p. 183 t.: Gerhard
Richter, Cologne.

Published by:
MONACO BOOKS is an imprint of Verlag Wolfgang Kunth

© Verlag Wolfgang Kunth GmbH & Co.KG, Munich, 2008
Concept: Wolfgang Kunth
Editing and design: Verlag Wolfgang Kunth GmbH & Co.KG
English translation: JMS Books LLP (translation Malcolm Garrard, editor Emma
Shackleton), design cbdesign, proofreader Jenni Davis, typesetter Kevin O'Connor)
For distribution please contact:
Monaco Books
C/o Verlag Wolfgang Kunth, Königinstr. 11
80539 München, Germany
Tel: +49/89/45 80 2- 23
Fax: +49/89/45 80 20 21
info@kunth-verlag. de
www.monacobooks.com
www.kunth-verlag.de

ISBN 978-3-89944-533-6
Printed in Slovakia

All facts are correct to the best of our knowledge. The editors and publishers cannot
however accept any responsibility for any inaccuracies. The publishers welcome
comments, suggestions or responses at any time.

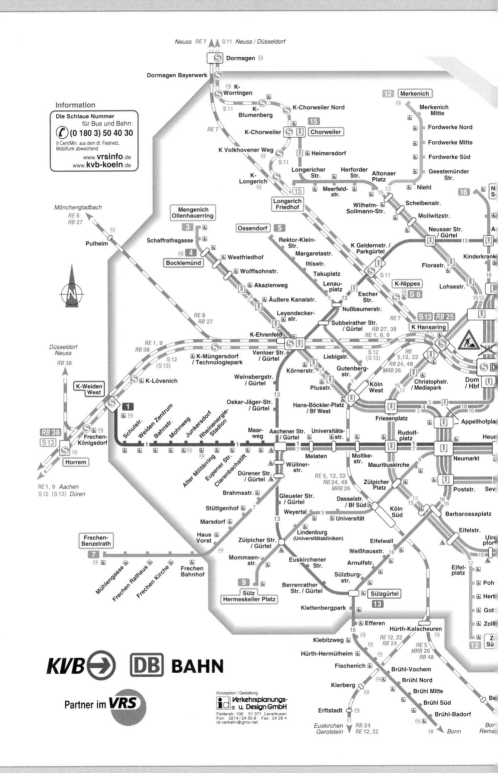